❤ **Healthy Living**
with

babies *and*
toddlers

Published in 2012 by Murdoch Books Pty Limited

Murdoch Books Australia
Pier 8/9
23 Hickson Road
Millers Point NSW 2000
Phone: +61 (0) 2 8220 2000
Fax: +61 (0) 2 8220 2558

www.murdochbooks.com.au
info@murdochbooks.com.au

Murdoch Books UK Limited
Erico House, 6th Floor North
6th Floor North
93–99 Upper Richmond Road
Putney, London SW15 2TG
Phone: +44 (0) 20 8785 5995
Fax: +44 (0) 20 8785 5985

www.murdochbooks.co.uk
info@murdochbooks.co.uk

For Corporate Orders & Custom Publishing contact Noel Hammond,
National Business Development Manager, Murdoch Books Australia

Publisher: Anneka Manning
Designer: Jacqueline Richards
Editor: Gabriella Sterio
Food Editor: Rebecca Truda
Nutritional consultants: Karen Kingham and Carol Fallows
Photographer: Ian Hofstetter
Stylists: Jane Collins
Food preparation: Joanne Kelly
Recipes by: Rebecca Truda and the Murdoch Books Test Kitchen
Project Editor: Martina Vascotto
Production: Alexandra Gonzalez

Text © Murdoch Books Pty Limited 2012
Design © Murdoch Books Pty Limited 2012
Photography copyright © Murdoch Books Pty Limited 2005

A cataloguing-in-publication entry is available from the catalogue of the National Library of Australia at www.nla.gov.au

A catalogue record for this book is available from the British Library.

Printed by 1010 Printing International Limited, China

IMPORTANT: Those who might be at risk from the effects of salmonella poisoning (the elderly, pregnant women, young children and those suffering from immune deficiency diseases) should consult their doctor with any concerns about eating raw eggs.

CONVERSION GUIDE: You may find cooking times vary depending on the oven you are using. For fan-forced ovens, as a general rule, set the oven temperature to 20°C (35°F) lower than indicated in the recipe. We have used 20 ml (4 teaspoon) tablespoon measures. If you are using a 15 ml (3 teaspoon) tablespoon, add an extra teaspoon for each tablespoon specified.

Healthy Living with
babies *and*
toddlers

EASY *healthy* RECIPES

MURDOCH BOOKS

contents

starting OUT

A good start to life includes a variety of tasty, healthy foods. By making an effort with baby's meals right from the start, you can establish the good habits your child will take with them into their future—a precious thing considering the number of diet-related diseases that face us in adulthood. Of course, there isn't always time for lengthy preparation, but this doesn't have to be the hallmark of a good meal.

Guidelines for introducing your baby to family foods are not set in stone. Most will start around 6 months, but every baby is different: some will show an interest in food before, others later. Follow your baby's cues for solids readiness. Ensure the best start, however, by not introducing any solids before 4 months.

first foods: from 6 months

In a baby's early days, food is a journey that's largely about taste, texture and smell. Your baby is still getting most of their vitamins, minerals and protein from milk. Theoretically, you can start your baby on almost any family food provided it's the right consistency—a smooth purée. However, you will have more success with relatively bland foods blended with the familiar flavour of breast milk or infant formula, such as an iron-fortified rice cereal. From here, move on to vegetables, fruits and meats.

introducing food

When first introducing solids to your baby, choose a time of day that suits you best. It might be after breakfast or before dinner, but you need to have time to take it gently and slowly; your baby needs to be relaxed and content.

Always give your baby milk before solids. Milk is still the most important source of nutrition, and it won't be replaced by food for another few of months.

For the first meal, offer just one to two teaspoons of smooth purée. If using rice cereal, mix it with expressed breast milk, formula or cooled boiled water. Remember, these first feeds need to have more of a smooth, runny consistency similar to pouring custard or yoghurt.

After a couple of days with one food, try another. In the beginning, it is important to offer new foods one at a time so that baby can learn about different tastes and textures and you can determine if there are any foods that do not agree with them (see pages 23–25 for details on the signs of food allergy and intolerance). As baby progresses with the amount and variety of solids, purées can also become more 'textured' and thicker.

If baby doesn't like a particular food, don't abandon it, try another and go back to it at a later date.

Avoid using added salt or sugar—even if the food appears bland or tasteless to you. Babies have 'new' tastebuds in high concentrations, so they taste flavours much more intensely than you.

making life easy

When you prepare baby's food, consider doing so in batches and freezing it to save time. Make enough to fill up half an ice cube

signs that your baby may be ready for solids:

- They hold things and put them in their mouth; they may try to grab food you are eating
- They can sit supported and hold their heads up
- They have lost the tongue-thrust reflex; if a spoon or your finger touches their tongue and it 'thrusts' the spoon or finger out, then they are not ready
- They seem to still be hungry after a milk feed and are not gaining weight; however, younger babies will go through periods like this, usually at around 6 weeks and 3–4 months, but this can be solved by offering them more breast milk or formula, not solids

avoid feeding your baby before they're ready because:

- It won't make them sleep better or sleep through the night; babies need to learn to sleep at night
- Giving solids too early can result in more fussiness with food later on
- They may not drink as much breast milk or formula as they need for optimum growth

tray; each cube is around 1 tablespoon. When you have done this a few times with a variety of different purées, you will have a well-stocked range of foods that you can thaw easily and combine together. Store frozen purée cubes in labelled and dated snap-lock bags.

Reheat frozen purées to steaming hot and then allow to cool. If you are using the microwave, stir food well before you test it on the inside of your wrist. Like formula, discard left-over food as it will contain bacteria-carrying saliva; never re-freeze or store it for later use.

introducing baby to drinking from a cup

Introduce your baby to a cup right from the start. A little water in a small, regular rimmed cup at meal times helps develop the healthy habit of water with meals. It may be messy at first, but babies are fast learners.

Spout or straw cups are great for when you are out and about, but avoid using them with meals or letting children carry them around all the time. Drinking from these types of cups is easy and children tend to fill up on fluids, which can dull hunger and lead to fussy eating at meals.

what to drink

The main source of fluid in the first 6 months should be either breast milk or infant formula. Over 6 months, babies will still enjoy breast milk or formula as their main drink. However, water and the occasional diluted fruit juice can also contribute to their total fluid intake.

There is no need to boil water for your baby once you start solids, and it's worth noting that bottled water does not contain fluoride (important for the healthy growth of baby's teeth). If you filter your water, check that the process does not remove the fluoride.

If offering juice, dilute it with one part juice to three parts water. Avoid using a bottle or spout cup for juice; use a rimmed cup, this way amounts can be kept small. Children over 12 months need no more than half a cup of diluted juice a day. Encourage them with fresh fruit and, if they're thirsty, a drink of water. Carbonated drinks, tea, coffee, cordial, flavoured milks and alcohol are not suitable for babies.

reasons your baby doesn't need juice:

o Its sugars can cause diarrhoea
o Too much can fill babies up and reduce their appetite for more nutritious foods
o It can cause tooth decay

first foods: from 7 months

Once baby is used to eating from a spoon and is having two or three solid meals a day, it is time to start making purées lumpier. This stage usually comes around 7–8 months.

Don't worry if there's no sign of teeth. Babies have hard gums and are able to chew. Try not to delay this stage as cheek and jaw muscles need the workout for later speech development. Research also shows that delays in texture can mean fussier eaters later on.

a growing appetite

Though milk is still important, begin giving food before the milk and start a routine for meal times. Breast milk or formula can be given when baby first wakes in the morning or after day-time naps and then again before bed at night.

Appetites will vary from baby to baby and so too will the size of their meals; never force baby to eat. It is better to serve too little food than too much. If baby is hungry, you can always offer more.

Finger foods can also be offered around this time. Babies love something to hold. Rusks (home-made or ready-made) can be popular even if they are not teething. Foods that dissolve or crush easily when they are sucked or chewed make ideal finger foods. Foods that are bitten off in hard lumps (such as carrot, apple or celery) are not ideal because of the risk of choking (see table on page 11).

Learning about texture doesn't just happen in the mouth. When your baby touches, squashes and spreads food with their hands, they are also learning about it. Try and relax with this behaviour, but if it gets too much for you, simply take the plate away without fuss.

Some babies are strongly independent and want to feed themselves. Two spoons work well in this situation: one for baby and one for you.

Avoid letting baby's growing independence with food take you away from the table. Babies still don't know their own limitations and can easily choke on seemingly appropriate finger foods. Always serve foods to baby in their high chair or sitting down on the floor or ground. Avoid letting them wander around with food.

foods not suitable for young children

honey	Because it can harbour spores of the bacteria *clostridium botulinum*, which produces toxins that can make babies very sick, honey is not recommended for babies and children under 12 months
tea, coffee or herbal teas	Tea and coffee, including decaffeinated coffee and some herbal teas, contain caffeine in varying amounts and are unsuitable for children. Herbal teas may also contain substances unsuitable for children
raw or undercooked egg	Raw or undercooked eggs pose a salmonella risk to infants and small children. Always cook eggs thoroughly
whole nuts, hard raw fruits and vegetables	These foods pose a significant choking risk to babies and children under 3 years. Serve hard fruits and raw vegetables thinly sliced, grated or lightly cooked to soften, and offer nuts only as a paste
cow's milk	Up until 12 months of age, breast milk or cow's milk-based formula is the best drink for babies. Cow's milk, along with goat's milk and sheep's milk, are poor sources of iron and also lack many of the other important nutrients— including vitamins A, C and E—that are found in breast milk and infant formulas
soy milk	Soy milk infant formula is not recommended for babies unless it has been prescribed for medical reasons. Soy milks and other cereal-based drinks are not a suitable substitute for cow's milk for children under 2 years.

Learning to eat can be a messy process. You can make this time easier on yourself if you think of it as an important and necessary learning experience for your baby. Placing baby's high chair on a plastic mat will also make it easier to clean up the inevitable mess.

first foods: from 9 months

This stage can emerge anywhere from 8 to 9 months. Breakfast, lunch and dinner routines become more established and you might also start to introduce snacks.

Food textures are coarser, lumpier, mashed, minced or cut up. Milk remains important but it is reduced as your baby's solid food intake increases to around half to one cup per meal.

By the time your baby reaches their first birthday, they will be eating many foods that the family normally eats, but it is still important to avoid hard foods, such as hard raw vegetables, fruits and whole nuts.

choking and gagging

Babies learn by putting things into their mouths. They will put anything that fits into their mouths and, consequently, choking is a major hazard for babies under two years of age (see table on page 11). But don't let the thought of your baby choking put you off giving soft finger foods. Your baby will learn to eat these foods, but in the process may gag.

A baby can gag on any food while learning to swallow and chew. A baby's gag reflex activates when they swallow too much, whether it is soft or hard. It is through gagging that babies learn how much is too much to swallow. Try not to panic when your baby gags. Wait for them to clear the food or hook it out with your finger if they have trouble.

toddler food: from 1 year

Independence is a feature of toddlers' behaviour, and meal times are a perfect time to show it. Appetites will wane as growth slows and fads and fussiness will come and go. Stay relaxed with food and your toddler will too. Finishing the plate is not what it is all about. Instead, trust your toddler to tell you when they are full. Make sure the food they get is good and healthy most of the time and you shouldn't have to worry about the adequacy of the nutrition they get.

tricks for trouble-free meal times

If you find your toddler is stubborn at meal times, there are things you can do to avoid a battle. Rest assured that you are not alone. These behaviours are part of a developmental stage and it's how you manage them that determines how disruptive they become. Here are some tips to stop them ruling your meal times:

- Look at your expectations. Are the meals you serve too large for your toddler's appetite? Expecting toddlers to eat more than they need will invariably end up in a battle.
- Eat as a family as often as you can. You are the most influential role model to your child. At this age, children are natural copycats and family meal times are an easy way to educate children about food and table manners. If you can't eat together, try to sit with your child, pull their chair up to the table and make it a special time. You need to be there to supervise.
- Offer the healthiest foods you can. This way you can be reassured that even if they eat only small amounts, they are still getting the best.
- Challenge food horizons. Continue to present new variations on food even if it's just a taste of your spicy Thai meal or curry. Some children take to lightly spiced food more quickly than others. Praise all attempts to try. Positive reinforcement for toddler behaviour is important.
- Set a good example. If you don't eat fruit and vegetables, you can't expect your child to. If you haven't been in the habit of getting your five vegetables and two or three pieces of fruit a day, then start now!
- Pick your battles. If your child refuses to eat something, take it away and offer it again another day. Don't get into battle.

breakfast

Your toddler needs breakfast, just as you do. Skipping breakfast contributes to poor concentration and forgetfulness. Those of us who eat breakfast tend to have better diets, so it's a good habit to instil in your children.

Mornings can be a challenge when everyone has to be ready on time. Consider these quick breakfast suggestions:

- Home-made muesli (granola) with yoghurt and fruit
- Quick-cook microwave oats (porridge)
- Fresh fruit salad with yoghurt
- Baked beans and toast fingers
- Fruit toast spread with ricotta or cream cheese
- Fruit and yoghurt smoothies
- Omelettes or scrambled eggs

Fresh is always best, but if it can't be fresh, stock up on alternatives. Frozen vegetables, fruit and fish make great nutritious and convenient substitutes for fresh.

lunch in a hurry

When kids are hungry, they often need food immediately. Consider these suggestions for a quick solution to a fast lunch:

- Microwave or bake a potato, cut it in half and serve it topped with a tin of no-added-salt baked beans or creamed corn
- Keep left-over pasta in the refrigerator to team with a tin of tuna or salmon plus any combination of the following: quartered cherry tomatoes, cooked frozen peas, tin sweet corn, grated cheese or avocado
- Mash up some avocado with cream cheese and serve with toast fingers for dipping
- Scrambled eggs or omelettes; don't just reserve these for breakfast
- Cheese and ham or tomato on toast

○ Cheat. You can hide vegetables in meat sauces, meatballs or casseroles. You can hide milk in sauces, custards or ice cream. Be creative. You can serve fish and chips (fries) on paper towels or in a clean takeaway food box, or wrap up a burger. You can make iceblocks (popsicles/ice lollies) out of frozen bananas on a stick, or smoothies from milk blended with fruit.

○ Involve them in the preparation. There are many simple things toddlers can do: fetch and carry anything unbreakable, wash vegetables or fruit, stir simple mixes and shake dressings.

○ Feed at around the same times each day. Toddlers are creatures of habit, so they like a routine.

○ Consider making lunch the main meal of the day. Toddlers are often tired at night, which exacerbates fussy behaviour. A substantial cooked meal at lunch takes the pressure off dinner for everyone.

○ Avoid food rewards for meals eaten. This tactic can actually make children dislike the food in question even more and place a heightened status to the reward food. Dessert is unnecessary if children eat enough of their main meal. If dessert is a regular feature, make it fruit or something dairy-based.

○ Trust your toddler's cues on hunger. If they don't want to eat, take food away without fuss. Don't be tempted to replace uneaten meals with favoured foods like pasta, fish fingers or nuggets. Children are fast learners and will use this strategy to get the foods they like at every meal.

○ No child will starve because they miss a meal. Remove uneaten food after a reasonable opportunity to eat it and remember that another meal or snack opportunity is never far away.

your family's food

Baby's nutrition needs are high, so every food needs to count Foods high in sugar and fat, such as chips (fries), sweet biscuits (cookies) or lollies (candy) contribute very little in the way of vitamins and minerals and take the place of foods that are more 'nutrient-dense'.

Use the following tips when you are shopping and cooking for the family as well as for your baby:

○ Think fresh. It is best to have fresh fruit and vegetables on hand. If you have a vegetable patch or fruit trees, you will have a great source of really fresh food. Even a few pots of fresh herbs on the window sill will be a bonus.

○ If it can't be fresh, stock up on frozen alternatives. Frozen vegetables, fruit and fish make great nutritious and convenient substitutes for fresh.

○ Make your own. It is easy and cheaper to make many of the basics, such as soups and salads—and you know exactly what they contain.

○ Read the labels (see pages 21–22 for more information). Some foods can contain ingredients that you may not normally suspect. For example, some breakfast cereals have more salt than potato chips (crisps).

○ Choose premium commercial baby foods. These foods make every parent's life easier, but as with all commercial foods, some will be better than others.

○ Use little or no salt and buy no-added-salt products. Babies and children do not need salt. You can always add salt or condiments to your own meal later, but it is not possible to take it out.

○ Avoid sweetened food. Children can learn to enjoy the natural sweetness of food without adding more.

○ Choose foods low in saturated fat, but don't give your baby or toddler low-fat foods. This may sound like a contradiction, but it isn't. Children under two years need healthy fat in their diet. Foods lower in saturated fat include chicken without the skin, lean meat, whole dairy products, legumes, vegetable oils, margarines, avocado, nuts and nut pastes.

dinner

Tiredness is often an issue at dinnertime. Don't delay dinner, if it can be helped, as an overtired and emotional toddler is not likely to eat, even if they are hungry. Don't be afraid to use convenience foods to make life quicker and easier; just check the label for unwanted extras (see pages 21–22 for more information). Try the following ideas:

○ Microwaved (or steamed) fresh or frozen fish served with a cooked frozen vegetable medley

○ Pasta with sliced ham, cooked frozen peas and grated cheese

○ Scrambled eggs and oven-fried potato chips (French fries)

○ Boil up some fresh quick-cook Asian noodles with a frozen vegetable medley and serve with shredded barbecued (grilled) chicken tossed through

○ Couscous with tin tuna or salmon and frozen vegetable medley

○ Macaroni cheese (see the recipe on page 68)

Introducing Food to babies: A parent's Quick Guide*

	Around 6 months	From 7 months	9–12 months	12 months +**
Milk feeds	Offer before solids; breast feed on demand or around 600 ml (21 fl oz) infant formula over 4–5 feeds per day	Breast feed on demand or around 600ml (21 fl oz) infant formula over 3–4 feeds per day	Breast feed on demand or around 600 ml (21 fl oz) infant formula over 3 feeds per day	Breast feed on demand
Texture	Smooth purée to start, then progressing to coarser purée and finely mashed foods	Finely mashed food graduating to coarse mash and lumpy consistencies	Mashed, minced and soft, cut up finger foods	Family foods modified for texture and low in salt
Progression	Build variety with one new food at a time and watch for reactions.			
Amount and frequency	1–2 teaspoons once a day, gradually increasing to 1 or more tablespoons twice to three times a day	Two tablespoons to ½ cup as part of three 'meals' a day	Half to one cup as part of a breakfast, lunch and dinner routine. Start to introduce snacks close to 12 months	Eat to appetite from 3 meals and 2–3 snacks each day. Use the information below as a guide. Remember, children may differ in the amounts they eat from day to day
Cereal grains, rice, oats, barley, wheat, corn	Purée with expressed breast milk, infant formula or cool boiled water; plain cereals such as rice, oats, semolina and polenta	Rolled oats, pasta, noodles, steamed rice, cous cous, polenta, bulgur, barley, semolina, quinoa, unsweetened adult breakfast cereals	Bread, toast, crackers; wholemeal (whole-wheat), wholegrain, white, rye, etc	4 serves per day where 1 serve is equal to 1 slice of bread, crumpet or English muffin, ½ cup cooked rice, pasta, noodles, polenta, porridge, barley, semolina, quinoa, 2/3 cup breakfast cereal flakes or ¼ cup muesli
Vegetables	Offer cooked vegetables individually to start. Avoid adding salt	Continue to cook and lightly mash or coarsely blend a variety of vegetables	Grated raw vegetables or soft, cooked, cut up pieces	2–3 serves per day where one serve is equal to ½ cup cooked vegetables or legumes or 1 cup raw leafy vegetables
Fruits	Offer cooked fruits individually to start. Avoid adding sugar	Raw soft fruits such as banana, avocado, soft pear, watermelon and summer fruits. Continue to cook hard fruits and lightly mash	Cooked or grated raw hard fruits or cut up pieces of soft, raw fruits, peeled and seeded	½ serve a day where one serve is equal to 1 medium piece of fruit, 2 small pieces of fruit, 1 cup diced cooked or canned fruit, 125 ml (4 fl oz) fruit juice or 30 g (1 oz) dried fruit

Introducing Food to babies: A parent's Quick Guide*

	Around 6 months	From 7 months	9-12 months	12 months +**
Meat and seafood	Use a food processor or stick blender with boiled water or casserole juices for the best texture	Coarse purée or moist minced meat and seafood	Minced or cut up pieces of moist cooked meat and seafood	1 serve per day where one serve is equal to ½ cup lean mince, 2 small chops, 2 slices roast meat, 80 g (2¾ oz)cooked chicken, 100 g (3½ oz) cooked fish or 1 small can, 2 large eggs, 1 cup legumes, 170 g (6 oz) tofu or 30 g (1 oz) nuts or nut paste
Legumes and pulses	Purée with cooking water, expressed breast milk, formula or other fruit, vegetable or cereal purées	Fork-mash softer beans and pulses	Soft, cooked whole beans and pulses	
Eggs	Cooked in custards or purées. Avoid all raw or undercooked egg.	Scrambled egg, fork-mashed as needed. Avoid all raw or undercooked egg.	Scrambled egg, cut up; hard boiled eggs, omelettes and frittatas. Avoid all raw or undercooked egg.	
Nuts	Nut pastes; avoid whole nuts and watch for allergic reactions	Nut pastes; avoid whole nuts	Nut pastes; avoid whole nuts	
Cow's milk	Whole milk cooked into custards and sauces	Whole milk cooked into food or added to breakfast cereal	Offer whole milk as a drink after 12 months	1–1.5 serves per day where 1 serve is equal to 250 ml (9 fl oz) milk, 2 slices cheese or 200 g (7 oz) tub yoghurt
Cheese	Regular (not low fat) added to other puréed foods	Added to other cooked foods	Grated, cut into sticks, sliced on sandwiches or grilled on toast	
Yoghurt	Regular (not low fat or diet) and natural, combined with other pureed foods	Served plain or combined with other foods	Served plain or combined with other foods	
Drinks	Small amount of tap water from a rimmed cup	Tap water from a rimmed cup or spout cup when out	Tap water from a rimmed cup or spout cup or small amounts of diluted fruit juice (1 part juice to 3 parts water) from a rimmed cup	Water or milk as main drinks

* Based upon *Draft Infant Feeding Guidelines for Health Workers* (2011)
**Based on *Draft Dietary Guidelines: The Australian Guide to Healthy Eating* (2011)

important nutrients

Baby's stores of iron and zinc deplete around the age of 6 months, and milk feeds can't support increased requirements. Commercial, iron-enriched baby rice cereals and lean meat purées can help top up falling iron stores.

A variety of fruit, vegetables, grains, legumes, meat, fish, eggs and nuts will provide your baby with new textures and tastes as well as important vitamins and minerals, fats and protein.

Ensure your baby spends some time exposed to gentle, indirect sunlight to provide enough vitamin D to meet their needs.

For an overview of the food sources of important nutrients, refer to the chart on pages 28–29.

including nutrients

There are many practical ways to ensure important nutrients are included in your family's diet, such as:

○ Eat a wide range of breads, including wholegrain and wholemeal (whole-wheat), cereals, rice, pasta and noodles, cous cous and quinoa. From these foods come fibre, vitamins, minerals, carbohydrates and protein.

○ Choose a wide variety of vegetables and legumes. No-added-salt tin and frozen are good alternatives when fresh are not available. Important vitamins, minerals, dietary fibre and carbohydrates are found in vegetables, beans, lentils and other legumes. When planning a family meal, a simple way to include a wide variety of vitamins and minerals is to include one white, one red or yellow and one green vegetable.

○ Eat enough fruit and choose whole fruit instead of juice. Dried fruits are a nutritious alternative, as are tin and frozen fruit without any added sugar. Fruit provides vitamins, including vitamin C and folate, carbohydrates and fibre.

○ Offer whole milk, yoghurt and cheese, all of which are valuable sources of calcium, protein, riboflavin and vitamin B12. You don't have to drink milk and eat cheese—you can add milk to soups, casseroles and sauces. Include cheese in dishes such as omelettes and vegetable dishes, and use yoghurt in curries and dips. Low- and reduced-fat dairy products are not suitable for babies and toddlers under the age of 2 years. Other sources of calcium include tin fish (with the bones), soy milk, lentils, almonds, brazil nuts and dried apricots.

- Include a variety of lean red meat, fish, poultry, eggs and legumes in the diet. These foods provide valuable protein, iron and zinc. Red meat is particularly high in these nutrients and, along with fish, supplies healthy omega 3 fats. Nuts are an important source of minerals and healthy fats, but avoid whole nuts in children under 3 because as they are a choking hazard. Smooth nut butters or crushed nuts are fine for children to consume.
- If you are vegetarian, legumes, seeds and nuts, as well as wholegrain cereals and breads, are important and should be teamed with fruit or vitamin C rich vegetables to maximise the absorption of important minerals such as iron.

the vegetarian or vegan baby

Vegetarian babies can be introduced to solid foods in much the same way as babies whose families eat meat. Replace smooth purées of meat with foods rich in plant protein, such as tofu, and soaked and well cooked dried peas and beans. Avoid canned varieties as these contain added salt. Pairing these foods with those rich in vitamin C helps baby absorb their valuable iron.

Milk, cheese and eggs also provide valuable and easy to digest protein, as does breast milk or infant formula. It is recommended that vegetarian or vegan babies are breast fed for two years or more if possible.

If you plan to feed your baby a vegan diet, seek the advice of a dietitian or doctor as nutritional supplements, particularly vitamin B12, might be necessary.

organic food

Organic foods have been produced without the use of synthetic fertilisers, pesticides or other chemicals. They are not genetically modified and irradiation is prohibited. When a food is organically certified, it means that not only has it been organically grown, but that it has also been harvested, prepared and transported using systems that guarantee the produce is not contaminated by synthetic chemicals.

Organic baby food is one of the biggest growth areas for organic farmers in many countries. However, you need to be aware that these foods may contain small amounts of non-organic ingredients—these will be specified on the label.

Organic food is more expensive than regular food because it

simple snacks

Your toddler needs to eat at least five times a day, so think of the snacks you give them as a mini meal rather than a time for traditional 'snack' foods. Healthy snacks for toddlers include:

- Grape or cherry tomatoes with cheese cubes
- Mini home-made muffin and some grapes
- Popcorn and sultanas
- Half a peanut butter sandwich and some apple slices
- Half a tub of yoghurt and some strawberries
- Cold hard-boiled egg and a glass of milk

Sugar is not bad for children when it comes naturally, as it does in fruit and milk, or when small amounts of it accompany healthy foods, such as dairy or high-fibre grain-based foods such as breakfast cereals.

costs more to produce. This can make organic food unaffordable for many families. Looking for bargains, using your freezer, buying food when it is in season, buying frozen organic vegetables if they are cheaper than the non-frozen variety and growing your own food and are some of the ways you can provide your family with a diet based on organic foods if this is important to you.

commercial baby food

Baby food that is tinned, jarred, in sachets or frozen can be a saviour when you are in a hurry, things are not going to plan, you have to go out or you are away from home.

Regulated by strict standards with regards to the addition of sugar, salt, preservatives and additives, premium commercial baby food is safe and nutritious and, in many cases, can offer the next best thing to home cooked food. Do avoid abusing the convenience, however; baby food from a squeeze pouch is not an acceptable snack for a toddler. Toddlers also don't need to eat specially formulated and marketed children's food or drinks. Provided you are choosing healthy convenient options for the whole family, they can eat what you are eating.

For more information on how to get the best for your baby and toddler off the shelf, check the section on reading labels (page 21).

quick meal solutions

Feeding hungry young children and babies when they want food instantly is never easy. Here are some quick options you might already have to hand:

O Team mashed fruits with ricotta cheese, avocado or thick plain yoghurt.

birthdays & other occasions
Celebrating doesn't have to mean unhealthy food, as you will find out in our *Desserts and party food* chapter. Foods with crunch, colour and sweetness can all be tasty and good for your child too. It's important to establish a good treat policy for your family. To deny children treat foods only heightens their desire for them and creates unhealthy fixations. Serve up nutritious foods at parties and other special occasions, but don't forget the treats too!

- No-added-salt baked beans is an excellent stand-by meal for older babies, or serve them with toast fingers for toddlers.
- Water-packed tin fish (salmon, tuna, sardines, mackerel) all mash and flake well—just crush or remove any bones (which are usually very soft anyway).
- Avocado, banana, mango, papaya, pear or kiwi fruit take very little time to prepare and require no cooking.
- It also takes no time at all to beat an egg and make an omelette. See our recipe for this basic and nourishing meal on page 65.

read the label!

A lot can be learned from reading the ingredients list on a product's label. The ingredient in the greatest quantity will come first and so on down to the last ingredient. If you find ingredients that you wouldn't normally put into your own version of a baby food, such as starches or other cereals, it is likely they may be used to bulk the meal out, so consider another brand. You should also consider the following:

- If the food's name is based on ingredients such as 'sweet corn and chicken', then the manufacturer is obliged to state what percentage these ingredients are of the final food. High-quality baby foods will do this with all their ingredients so you know exactly what you are feeding your baby.
- In most countries, the information panel will tell you about the energy, fat, saturated fat, protein, carbohydrate, sugar and sodium content of the food 'per serve' and/or 'per 100 g (3½ oz)'. Using the 'per 100 g (3½ oz)' column, if it is present, makes comparing food products easy. Other nutrients may also be on the panel, but those listed above should always be there. For more information on food labels and how to use them, contact your local government food authority.
- When shopping for young children, consider the amount of sodium and sugar in food. Fat might be an issue for the family as whole, but low-fat foods are not appropriate for young children.
- Sodium is part of sodium chloride or salt. Commercial foods can be high in salt. The easiest way to keep salt to a minimum in your family's diet is to look for products labelled no-added-salt, reduced-salt or low-salt. Alternatively, compare similar products and choose the one with the lowest amount of sodium.

○ Sugar is not bad for children when it comes naturally, as it does in fruit and milk, or when small amounts of it accompany healthy foods, such as dairy or high-fibre grain-based foods such as breakfast cereals. You can keep extra sugar out of your family's diet by choosing foods with no-added-sugar, reduced-sugar or low-in-sugar on the label. Because sugar comes naturally from fruit-based ingredients, using your judgement based on the ingredients list and the information on the nutrition label is often best. For example, it is unlikely a fruit-based food will ever be labelled 'low sugar', but this doesn't mean that it won't be healthy if it has no added sugars and just contains the natural sugars from the fruit.

○ 'No artificial colours, flavours or preservatives' is something that you may find on the labels of food marketed for children. Be aware that it is not only the artificial ones that can cause problems for children. That said, the majority of the additives used in the world's food supply are necessary to ensure food is safe for us to eat. If you are concerned about additives in your child's diet, see the allergy and intolerance section in this book (page 23–25) for information.

food safety

Bacteria and viruses can cause food-borne illness in children and adults. It's not always possible to tell by the way food looks, smells or tastes whether or not it contains pathogens. Being careful and hygienic will help prevent food poisoning, which can be a very serious illness in babies. Other tips include:

○ Shop for non-perishables first and put cold foods in an insulated bag.

○ Put raw meats in separate bags from other foods.

○ Avoid foods in damaged packaging.

○ Unpack and refrigerate perishables as soon as you arrive home.

○ Make sure your refrigerator is between 4–5°C (39–41°F); and your freezer is between -15 and -18°C (59–65°F).

○ Thaw frozen food in the refrigerator or microwave rather than the kitchen bench or chopping board.

○ Always wash hands with warm soapy water before preparing food and in between tasks.

- Do not prepare family food if you have had vomiting or diarrhoea.
- Use separate chopping boards and utensils for cooked and raw foods, and wash them in hot soapy water.
- Be sure the food you cook is completely cooked through. This is particularly important for poultry and minced (ground) meat—juices should run clear when poultry is pierced with a skewer.
- Cool hot food quickly. Put it into the refrigerator as soon as the steam has stopped rising.
- Store cooked leftovers in the refrigerator and throw away if not used within two days.
- Always reheat food to steaming hot. If you are using a microwave, be sure to stir the food during reheating. If it is for baby, taste it with a separate spoon.
- Don't use the same plate for raw and cooked food.
- Thoroughly wash and dry all fruit and vegetables.
- Discard cracked or damaged eggs.
- Wash all working surfaces with warm soapy water.
- Change tea towels (dish towels) and dishcloths regularly—at least every couple of days. Disposable paper towels are a good alternative.
- Wash your baby's hands before and after they eat.
- Never mix pet dishes with your own. Wash and dry them separately.

food allergy

Food allergy is an abnormal reaction by the immune system to proteins found in food, and one of the defining characteristics of food allergy is the almost instant symptoms that occur when the offending food is eaten.

Foods most likely to cause an allergic reaction have, in the past, been delayed in the progression of solids introduction because of the belief that it may prevent the development of food allergy. What we know today is there is no benefit to avoiding potentially allergenic foods and that to delay their introduction may actually increase your baby's allergy risks. These recommendations remain unchanged for babies with a strong family history of allergy. However, it is recommended that these babies are exclusively breast fed for their first 6 months, and

listeria

Listeria is bacteria that can cause serious illness in some people if they eat food that is contaminated with it. In the early days of starting new foods, babies are particularly susceptible.

Your baby has plenty of years ahead in which to eat the foods listed below, so for now it is wise not to include them in their diet. Foods that have a high risk of containing listeria are:

- Ready-to-eat, sliced cold meats from delicatessens
- Cold, cooked takeaway chicken
- Pâté and meat spreads
- Ready-made fruit or vegetable salads from salad bars
- Raw shellfish and smoked seafood
- Soft, semi-soft and unripened cheeses such as camembert, brie, fetta, ricotta and blue cheese
- Soft-serve ice cream
- Unpasteurised dairy products

that breast feeding must continue throughout the period of solids introduction.

New foods should be introduced one at a time whilst watching carefully for reactions. Symptoms of food allergy in young children include swelling, particularly around the mouth, hives, rashes and eczema. Less common is diarrhoea, vomiting, wheezing or asthma. Severe allergies can result in the potentially fatal state of anaphylaxis.

The good news for allergic children is that many will outgrow their food allergy by the time they go to school. Allergies most likely to remain are those to peanut or other nuts and fish; these tend to be lifelong.

There may be many other causes for the types of symptoms seen in food allergy, so it is recommended that you seek expert help. Treatment of a true food allergy requires complete exclusion of the food or food group from the diet. For young children, this needs the specialised help of a dietitian to make sure their diet is adequate for their growth and development.

food intolerance

Food intolerances are reactions to the chemicals found in food— both natural and added. These reactions, unlike food allergy, are not a response by the immune system, but are instead thought to be the result of irritation to nerve endings. Unlike allergy, the symptoms of food intolerance are very rarely associated with the food most recently consumed. Symptoms of food intolerance come about when tolerance thresholds for 'culprit chemicals; are reached. As such, they may occur many hours after the offending food/s were eaten.

Foods likely to cause intolerance in sensitive children are those rich in the natural chemicals salicylate, amine and glutamate. The list of these foods is quite extensive, so it is easier to consider those which are least likely to cause a problem (see list on page 24). Many of these 'lower chemical' foods can be given as first foods with higher chemical foods being introduced a little later.

Added chemicals (see box on page 25) can also be problematic for sensitive children and may result in emotional and behavioural symptoms. Because foods containing added

Food additives most likely to cause an adverse reaction	
Colours	102, 107, 110, 122-129, 132, 133, 142, 151, 155, 160B (natural)
Preservatives	200–203, 210–218, 220–228, 249–252, 280–283, 310–312, 319–321
Flavour enhancers	620–635, hydrolysed vegetable protein (HVP), textured vegetable protein (TVP)

chemicals don't feature highly in the diets of babies or younger toddlers, they are more likely to be an issue in three and four year-olds.

Food intolerance symptoms are wide ranging and include the rashes, eczema and hives seen in food allergy, as well as colic, diarrhoea, nappy rash, vomiting and generalised irritability. Once again, because these symptoms could have many other causes, it is important to have your child seen by an expert before restricting their diet. Treatment of food intolerances is complex and may require complete or only partial elimination of problem foods from the diet. A dietitian specialising in food allergy and intolerance is best qualified to give you this advice.

Foods most likely to cause an allergic reaction:

o Eggs
o Cow's milk
o Peanuts and other nuts
o Soy
o Wheat
o Fish and shellfish
o Sesame

lactose intolerance

The natural sugar in all kinds of milk is known as lactose. It is an important source of energy for babies. Lactase is the enzyme in the digestive system that helps to break down the lactose in milk. When not enough of this enzyme is present, the digestive system cannot cope and lactose intolerance results, which can manifest in bloating, tummy pain and diarrhoea.

In babies and young children, lactose intolerance is not common except as a result of gastroenteritis and other diarrhoea-causing illnesses. This type of lactose intolerance is only temporary and for the formula-fed baby a lactose free formula can be given for a few weeks. Breastfed babies should continue to breastfeed. For toddlers, the removal of high lactose foods like milk, yoghurt and ice cream is usually recommended. Lactose-free milk and processed hard cheeses are lactose-reduced alternatives that can be used until lactose tolerance returns.

choosing a high chair

A high chair is a major piece of equipment. There are safety and ease-of-use issues with high chairs, so look for one that:

- Has a five-point harness to prevent your child from falling or climbing out
- Is strong but lightweight. Lean on it to check its strength. Does it sag, squeak or buckle?
- Has no sharp edges and is without removable pieces that could find their way into your child's mouth
- Fits into your kitchen, family room or around your table. If the legs stick out, will you trip over them?
- Has a tray that is well secured when in place, but can be easily removed for cleaning
- Can be adjusted for height. Also, check if the seat reclines—not all highchairs recline, but this mechanism can be useful. Any adjustment knobs should be out of a child's reach when they are sitting in the highchair
- Folds away easily, ideally with one hand. If space is a problem, folding it up quickly and being able to lift it will be important.
- Has an adjustable leg rest for your child.
- Is quite easy to wipe down

necessary equipment

As with most items specifically designed for babies, you can spend a lot of money on eating equipment. In reality, however, you will only need one or two bowls and several flat spoons. You can add a baby fork at a later date. You will also want enough bibs, so you can wash or soak some while your baby wears others. The ideal bib covers your baby's shoulders and stomach. Have a few cups with non-spill features; they are extremely useful once your baby learns that drinks go into his tummy, not on the floor, the high chair, or on your lap. If you have sterilising equipment for bottles, you can use this for baby spoons and beaker spouts. Otherwise, clean utensils thoroughly in hot soapy water or use the dishwasher. You may also want to consider a mess mat, which you will need to clean at the end of every meal.

Sources of Major Nutrients

Nutrient	Food sources	Important for
Protein	Breast milk, infant formula, lean meats, fish, seafood, poultry, eggs, dairy foods, legumes, grains, nuts and seeds	Growth and repair of all body cells. Children have a proportionally greater need for protein than adults because they are growing and protein is needed for the formation of new cells
Fat	Breast milk, infant formula, oils, margarine, lean meats, fish, eggs, dairy foods, whole grains, olives, avocados, nuts and seeds	General health and the absorption of fat-soluble vitamins A, D, E and K. Fats are also an important stored source of energy/fuel for growing babies and toddlers. This is because of their small stomachs and high needs for energy
Essential fatty acids (omega-3 fats)	Breast milk, some infant formula, lean meats, fish, canola, sunflower and safflower oils and margarine, linseeds (flax seeds), walnuts, pecans and egg yolk	Brain and visual development, plus the production of hormone-like substances. Unlike other fats, these can't be made by the body, so they must come from food
Carbohydrates	Breast milk, infant formula, grains such as wheat, rice, oats, barley and foods made from them, such as bread, pasta, breakfast cereals, flour and semolina. Sugar, sweet corn, potato, root vegetables, fruit and milk	Supplying the body with its major source of energy. In their unprocessed forms, they are good sources of fibre
Fibre	Wholegrain breads and cereals, vegetables, fruits, legumes (dried peas and beans), nuts and seeds	Healthy, regular-functioning bowel
Vitamin A (retinol)	Breast milk, infant formula, dairy foods, liver, eggs, fortified margarine and oily fish	Well developed vision and healthy skin and hair
Beta-carotene	Orange and green fruit and vegetables, such as sweet potatoes, carrots, orange-fleshed melon, apricots, spinach and broccoli	Supply of vitamin A (beta-carotenes are converted into vitamin A in the body)
Thiamin (vitamin B1)	Breast milk, infant formula, wheat germ and wholemeal (whole-wheat) foods, yeast extracts, nuts, fortified breakfast cereals and lean pork	Release of energy from carbohydrate foods
Riboflavin (vitamin B2)	Breast milk, infant formula, dairy products, yeast extracts, meat extracts, eggs, fortified breakfast cereals, mushrooms, wholemeal (whole-wheat) flour and bread	Healthy skin and eye, and the release of energy from food
Niacin (vitamin B3)	Food source: Breast milk, infant formula, lean meats, peanuts, fish, legumes, fortified breakfast cereals, eggs, milk	Growth and release of energy from food

Sources of Major Nutrients

Nutrient	Food sources	Important for
Vitamin B12	Breast milk, infant formula, lean meats, chicken, fish, seafood, eggs, milk and fortified vegetarian products	Formation of nerve cells, genetic material (DNA) and red blood cells
Folic acid	Breast milk, infant formula, green leafy vegetables, whole grains, legumes, nuts and fortified breakfast cereals	Healthy growth and development, and the formation of red blood cells
Vitamin C	Breast milk, infant formula, potato, parsley, brussels sprouts, cabbage, capsicum (pepper), citrus fruits and juices, mango, berries and papaya	Healthy skin, bone and gums; helps the body absorb iron from foods other than meat
Vitamin D	Breast milk, infant formula, oily fish, eggs, butter, margarine and cheese	Absorption of calcium and phosphorus, and for strong and healthy teeth and bones. The body also makes this vitamin in the skin when it is exposed to sunlight
Vitamin E	Breast milk, infant formula, wheat germ and wheat germ oil, nuts, seeds and the oils of nuts and seeds	Development and maintenance of healthy body cells, especially in the blood and nervous systems, due to its antioxidant properties
Iodine	Breast milk, salt-water fish and seafood, kelp and seaweed, dairy foods, fortified bread and eggs	Regulation of physical and mental development
Iron	Breast milk, lean meats, chicken, fish, eggs, legumes, fortified baby cereals, wholegrain cereals, dark green leafy vegetables and dried fruits	Normal brain development, optimal immune function, healthy blood and muscles
Calcium	Breast milk, infant formula, dairy foods, calcium-fortified soy products, tin sardines and salmon (including bones)	Growth of strong and healthy bones and teeth
Fluoride	Fluoridated drinking water, fish	Strengthening teeth and reducing the risk of dental decay. Although not essential, the inclusion of fluoride in the diet is recommended by the World Health Organization (WHO)
Zinc	Breast milk, infant formula, lean meat, chicken, seafood, milk, legumes and nuts	Healthy growth, wound healing and immune system. Young children often don't get enough of this mineral

Developmental stages — A general guideline*

	reactions	hearing and speech	sight	hand movements	body movements and getting about
first weeks	6–8 weeks: first social smiles	Hears from birth. Cries from hunger and discomfort	Looks briefly at bright or close objects		When placed on stomach will turn head to side. Movements are jerky
2 months		Gurgling 'oos' and 'ahs'	Following with eyes		
3 months		Brief attention to sounds, including voices. Searches for sounds with eyes	Looking at faces and objects for longer periods of time	Holds objects that are placed in hands for short time	Can hold head steady for a period of time. When baby is propped in a sitting position, head tends to bob forward
4 months	Likes to be handled	Usually disturbed by angry voices. May utter sounds when spoken to or pleased. More consonants		Reaching out to get objects	Can hold head and chest up when lying on stomach, taking weight on forearms
5 months	Enjoys new tastes		Recognizes everyday objects, e.g. a cup. Watches hands		
6 months	May start to cling	Turns to sounds. Chuckles and babbles	Notices details in picture books. Recognizes familiar adults in photographs once they are pointed out	Objects put into mouth	Lifts head to look at feet. Sits with support. 6–8 months: rolling over
8 months	May cry when a parent goes out of sight. This may last past second birthday	Practising different sounds, e.g. 'googoo' and 'adada'	Sees small beads	7–8 months: able to transfer an object from one hand to another	

Developmental stages — A general guideline

	reactions	hearing and speech	sight	hand movements	body movements and getting about
9 months	Shy around strangers. Can cling to parents and hide face	Smacks lips together and may start to imitate adult noises, e.g. 'brr'			9–10 months: sits alone on floor for 10–15 minutes. Props to side or forwards to balance. Attempts to crawl (some children get around by bottom shuffling or wriggling and may walk later — up to 18 months). 10–18 months: first steps
10 months	Reacts to praise. Understands 'no'		Looks for objects dropped out of sight and finds toys hidden under a blanket	Beginning to use index finger and thumb to pick up small objects	
12 months		Understands some words and phrases. First words with meaning about this time, e.g. 'dada', 'mama'			12 months: pulls self to standing position and lets self down again, holding onto furniture
15 months	Dependant on adult's presence. Active and curious. Starting to explore. Emotionally 'up and down'	Starting to understand and obey simple commands such as 'get your shoes'. Using a few true words	Enjoys picture books. Points at named object	Picks up a lot of small objects using finger and thumb. Can throw things quite forcibly (this is still a game)	Can climb on furniture
18 months	Exploring energetically. Plays alone, but likes to be near adult. Emotionally still dependent on familiar adults	Using both noises and pointing to indicate what they want. Number of words increased		Can turn pages of a book one at a time	Around this time can usually walk quite well. Runs (with falls). Can climb stairs
2 years	Constantly seeks attention. Clings tightly in affection, fear or fatigue. Tantrums when frustrated	Speech becoming clearer. Puts two or more words together to form simple phrases, e.g. 'go shop'	Notices details in picture books. Recognises familiar adults in photographs once they are pointed out	Scribbles lines and rough circles. Feeds self with spoon	Starts to kick and can throw a ball. Very mobile and active

*First produced by the Paediatric Health Education Unit, University of Sydney

Baby food

Try pumpkin (winter squash) as a first vegetable for your baby. Its smooth, creamy texture and naturally sweet flavour makes it enjoyable for new palates.

Puréed vegetable

150 g (5½ oz/½ cup) vegetable such as finely chopped pumpkin (winter squash), potato, carrot, sweet potato, parsnip, peas, English spinach, broccoli or zucchini (courgette)

breast milk, formula or cooled boiled water

Prep time 5 minutes

Cooking time 15 minutes

Makes 6–8 serves

1 Put the chosen vegetable into a steamer basket over a saucepan of gently simmering water. Cover tightly and steam until tender.

2 Finely purée the vegetable pieces with a fork or press through a sieve. Add a little breast milk, formula or cooled boiled water to the mixture to achieve a smooth consistency.

3 After feeding, spoon the (untouched) remainder into ice cube trays and freeze or store in the refrigerator for up to 3 days.

variation If using tomatoes, peel and deseed them before passing them through a fine sieve.

puréed avocado Rich in healthy monounsaturated fats, avocado is also a good source of vitamin E and many of the B vitamins. This good nutrition, combined with its smooth, easy-to-prepare texture, means you have a perfect first food for babies. Choose a small, soft avocado. Mash or purée one-eighth of the avocado with breast milk, formula or cooled boiled water to achieve the desired consistency.

Oats provide all the goodness of a whole grain: carbohydrates for energy, plus vitamins, minerals, healthy fats and gentle fibre.

Baby oat porridge

25 g (1 oz/¼ cup) rolled (porridge) oats
185 ml (6 fl oz/¾ cup) milk

Prep time 5 minutes
Cooking time 5 minutes
Makes 3–4 serves

1 Grind the rolled oats to a fine powder in a spice grinder or a small food processor.

2 Put the oats in a small saucepan and gradually whisk in the milk and 60 ml (2 fl oz/¼ cup) water until well combined. Slowly bring to the boil and cook for 1–2 minutes, stirring constantly, or until the mixture thickens. Remove from the heat.

A bland food like rice cereal (either home-made or ready-made) is a good place to start the solids journey with your baby.

Ground rice cereal

40 g (1½ oz/¼ cup) short-grain polished rice
125 ml (4 fl oz/½ cup) water

1 Grind the rice to a smooth powder in a spice grinder or use a mortar and pestle.

2 Put in a small saucepan and stir in the water. Stir over low heat for 2–3 minutes, or until the mixture becomes thick and creamy.

bulk rice cereal Grind 220 g (7¾ oz/1 cup) short-grain polished rice to a smooth powder in a spice grinder or in a mortar with a pestle. Put in a small saucepan and stir in 625 ml (21½ fl oz/2½ cups) water. Stir over low heat for 2–3 minutes, or until the mixture becomes thick and creamy. Pour into ice cube trays and freeze.

Prep time 5 minutes
Cooking time 5 minutes
Makes 6 serves

A rich source of vegetable protein, lentils are an excellent food for babies. Ensure they are well cooked and consider including a little garlic and onion.

Lentils & vegetables

2 tablespoons lentils or split peas

2 tablespoons mashed mixed vegetables

milk or cooled boiled water

cottage cheese (optional)

Prep time 5 minutes

Cooking time 25 minutes

Makes 1 serve

1 Rinse the lentils or split peas under cold running water and drain. Bring a saucepan of water to the boil, add the lentils or split peas and cook for 20–25 minutes, or until tender.

2 Drain, then process in a blender or small food processor with the vegetables and a little milk or cooled boiled water to give a smooth consistency. Add a little cottage cheese if desired and mix well.

3 As baby gets older, simply mash the cooked ingredients together with a fork to produce a lumpier consistency.

chicken, lentils & vegetables Steam 1 boneless, skinless chicken tenderloin until cooked through. Add to the food processor with the lentils and vegetables and blend until smooth. As baby gets older and is starting to eat lumpier food, finely chop the steamed chicken and mash the cooked lentils and vegetables with a fork until lumpy, rather than pureé them.

Babies are born with an innate taste for sweet foods. The natural sweetness of fresh stewed fruits makes them great favourites.

Stewed fruit

1 medium apple, peach or pear, peeled, cored and sliced

1 Put the sliced fruit into a small saucepan with 2 tablespoons water. Bring to the boil, reduce the heat and simmer until soft and pulpy, adding more water as required.

2 Purée with a little boiled water to make about 125 ml (4 fl oz/½ cup) stewed fruit.

variations You can also use a variety of other fruits such as rhubarb or peeled and cored plums or apricots.

mashed banana Bananas are rich in vitamin C, which is an important nutrient to help boost baby's iron absorption. Choose a ripe banana. Mash or purée the banana with breast milk, formula or cooled boiled water to achieve the desired consistency.

Prep time 5 minutes
Cooking time 5 minutes
Makes 6–8 serves

Cauliflower, along with broccoli, brussels sprouts and cabbage, belong to the Brassica family of vegetables, which are all excellent sources of vitamin C.

Cauliflower soup

2 teaspoons olive oil

1 small brown onion, chopped

1 small garlic clove, crushed (optional)

300 g (10½ oz/2½ cups) cauliflower, cut into small florets

500 ml (17 fl oz/2 cups) water or salt-reduced vegetable or chicken stock

1 Heat the oil in a saucepan over medium heat. Add the onion and garlic and cook for 2–3 minutes, or until softened. Add the cauliflower and stock, cover and bring to the boil. Reduce the heat to low and simmer for 10 minutes. Cool slightly and process in a blender or food processor until smooth.

2 The soup keeps for up to 3 days in the refrigerator or can be frozen in serving-size portions for up to 2 months.

Prep time 10 minutes
Cooking time 15 minutes
Makes 6–8 serves

Iron is an important nutrient for babies and toddlers alike. Meals with iron-rich meats should be on the menu regularly to keep iron stores topped up.

Stewed beef & vegetables

90 g (3¼ oz) lean round or chuck
    steak or veal steak

1 small potato

1 small carrot

¼ small brown onion

½ garlic clove, crushed

small piece of bay leaf

sprig of parsley

1 Put the steak, potato, carrot and onion in a small saucepan. Add the garlic, the piece of bay leaf and parsley sprig, then cover with water. Cover, bring to the boil, then simmer gently until the meat is tender. Add more water as needed.

2 Discard the bay leaf and parsley. Blend the ingredients with a little of the cooking liquid.

Prep time 5 minutes
Cooking time 40 minutes
Makes 2 serves

White fish has a soft texture and mild flavour that your baby should enjoy. Fish is rich in high-quality protein, plus vitamins and minerals such as vitamin D and iodine, which are important for growth and development.

Poached fish with potato & peas

60 g (2¼ oz) piece boneless
   white fish

milk

1 small new potato, cut into cubes

2 teaspoons frozen peas

Prep time 10 minutes
Cooking time 5 minutes
Makes 1 serve

1 Put the fish in a small saucepan and add enough milk to cover. Simmer, covered, for 3–5 minutes, or until tender.

2 Meanwhile, add the potato and peas to boiling water and cook until tender. Drain. Mash the potato and peas, adding a little milk from the fish.

3 Remove any bones from the fish, then flake and serve with the mashed vegetables or mix through the vegetables.

The mild flavour of chicken teams well with the sweetness of fruit. Using a fruit that your baby is familiar with helps to introduce them to a new flavour.

Steamed chicken & apple

½ red cooking apple, peeled and cored

2 chicken tenderloins

1 Thinly slice the apple and cut the chicken into small cubes. Place the chicken tenderloin pieces in a steamer and arrange the apple slices over the chicken. Set over a saucepan of boiling water and steam for about 5 minutes, or until tender.

2 Purée or finely chop the chicken and apple with a little of the cooking liquid.

Prep time 10 minutes
Cooking time 5 minutes
Makes 1 serve

As babies discover their hands, they will want to use them to get everything within reach to their mouth. Offering a rusk when this happens will launch your baby into the world of finger food.

Homemade rusks

1 loaf unsliced wholemeal (whole-wheat) bread

Prep time 10 minutes
Cooking time 1 hour
Makes about 80

1 Preheat the oven to 130°C (250°F/Gas 1). Cut the bread into 2.5 cm (1 inch) thick slices. Remove the crusts and cut each slice into strips about 1.5 cm (½ inch) wide.

2 Bake the strips on an ungreased baking tray for about 1 hour, or until the rusks are dry and crisp. Turn them over occasionally.

3 Cool and store in an airtight container for up to 7 days.

yeast extract & cheese rusks Preheat the oven to 150°C (300°F/Gas 2). Spread slices of day-old bread with yeast extract and cover with a thin layer of grated cheddar cheese. Cut into fingers and bake for 1½–2 hours until really hard. Store these rusks in an airtight container.

Eggs are a good source of protein and fat, as well as valuable vitamins and minerals. In fact, they contain every nutrient except vitamin C, making them an important part of a growing baby's diet.

Simple scrambled eggs

1 whole egg

1 egg yolk

1 tablespoon milk

1 teaspoon vegetable oil or margarine

1 Lightly beat together the whole egg and egg yolk with the milk. Heat the oil or margarine in a small non-stick frying pan over low heat and pour in the egg mixture. Cook, stirring occasionally, until the egg begins to set underneath. This will take about 3–4 minutes. Stir lightly and cook until just set. Serve the scrambled eggs puréed or fork-mashed for younger babies, or with lightly toasted bread for older babies.

variations Try adding grated cheese and chopped cooked chicken for a more substantial meal. Alternatively, fold through finely chopped wilted baby English spinach leaves and finely chopped tomatoes.

Prep time 2 minutes

Cooking time 4 minutes

Makes 1 serve

It's not just babies who need to eat fish. Health authorities recommend that we all should have at least one or two fish meals a week.

Steamed fish & diced vegetables

60 g (2¼ oz) piece boneless white fish, cut into cubes

2 tablespoons finely diced vegetables (asparagus, broccoli, carrot, frozen peas)

milk (optional)

Prep time 10 minutes

Cooking time 8 minutes

Makes 1 serve

1 Put the fish with the vegetables in a steamer and set over a saucepan of boiling water. Steam for about 8 minutes, or until tender.

2 Mash the fish and vegetables together to form a smooth consistency, adding a little of the cooking liquid or milk if necessary. Otherwise, flake the fish and chop the accompanying vegetables, adding a little milk or cooking liquid.

This recipe uses vegetables that your baby knows, and it is their start on family foods. Blend it in the early stages of baby's feeding development, if necessary.

Carrot & pumpkin risotto

90 g (3¼ oz) unsalted butter

1 brown onion, finely chopped

250 g (9 oz) pumpkin (winter squash), cut into small cubes

2 carrots, cut into small cubes

1.75–2 litres (61–70 fl oz/7–8 cups) salt-reduced vegetable stock

440 g (15½ oz/2 cups) arborio rice

90 g (3¼ oz/1 cup) freshly grated parmesan cheese

¼ teaspoon ground nutmeg

Prep time 15 minutes
Cooking time 35 minutes
Makes 4 serves

1 Heat 60 g (2¼ oz) of the butter in a large, heavy-based saucepan. Add the onion and fry for 1–2 minutes, or until soft. Add the pumpkin and carrot and cook for 6–8 minutes, or until tender. Mash slightly with a potato masher. Put the stock in a separate saucepan and keep at simmering point.

2 Add the rice to the vegetables and cook for 1 minute, stirring constantly. Ladle in enough hot stock to cover the rice; stir well. Reduce the heat and add more stock as it is absorbed, stirring frequently. Continue until the rice is tender and creamy (this will take about 25 minutes).

3 Remove the pan from the heat, add the remaining butter, cheese and nutmeg and season with freshly ground black pepper. Fold through. Cover and leave for 5 minutes before serving.

hint Left-over risotto is great the next day formed into balls and deep-fried. Ensure the balls are cool before serving them to baby.

When well cooked, this dish makes a creamy meal for younger babies. With less cooking, the firm florets make an ideal finger food for the older baby.

Cauliflower in creamy sauce

60 g (2¼ oz) fresh or frozen cauliflower, cut into small florets

2 tablespoons milk

1 teaspoon dry milk powder or ricotta cheese

¾ teaspoon cornflour (cornstarch)

1 Cut the cauliflower into small florets and boil or steam until tender. Drain well.

2 Put the milk, milk powder or ricotta cheese and cornflour in a small saucepan. Cook, stirring, until thickened.

3 Finely chop or mash the cauliflower and stir into the sauce.

hint This recipe can also be used for diced carrots, tiny florets of broccoli, diced asparagus or pumpkin (winter squash).

Prep time 5 minutes

Cooking time 8 minutes

Makes 1 serve

Rich with flavour, this dish is well worth the time. It is also big on protein, iron, zinc and soluble barley fibre (the gentle type).

Lamb shank & barley casserole

1 tablespoon olive oil

1 small brown onion, finely chopped

1 garlic clove, crushed (optional)

50 g (1¾ oz/⅓ cup) diced carrot

2 tablespoons finely diced celery

2 teaspoons finely chopped rosemary

2 French trimmed lamb shanks
   (about 600 g/1 lb 5 oz)

plain (all-purpose) flour, for dusting

2 tablespoons pearl barley

500 ml (17 fl oz/2 cups) salt-reduced
   beef stock

Prep time 15 minutes

Cooking time 2 hours 10 minutes

Makes 3–4 serves

1   Heat the oil in a small flameproof casserole dish or heavy-based saucepan. Add the onion, garlic, carrot, celery and rosemary and cook over medium heat for about 5 minutes, or until soft.

2   Dust the lamb shanks in flour, shaking off any excess. Add to the dish, turning to brown all sides. Add the barley and stock and bring to the boil. Reduce the heat to low and cook, covered, for 2 hours, or until the meat is very tender and falling away from the bone.

3   Remove the shanks, allow to cool slightly, then remove the meat from the bone, discarding any sinew. Cut the meat into small pieces and return to the casserole, stirring to combine. For a smoother texture, put in a food processor and lightly process. This meal can be frozen for up to 3 months. Thaw, then reheat to serve.

Lentils are a powerhouse of nutrition. Excellent as a source of protein, iron and zinc, they provide a valuable alternative to meat.

Dhal

310 g (11 oz/1¼ cups) red lentils

1 tablespoon vegetable oil

1 medium brown onion, finely
  chopped

2 garlic cloves, crushed

1 teaspoon grated fresh ginger

1 teaspoon ground turmeric

1 teaspoon garam masala

Prep time 15 minutes

Cooking time 20 minutes

Makes 4–6 serves

1 Put the lentils in a large bowl and cover with water. Remove any floating particles and drain the lentils well.

2 Heat the oil in a saucepan. Fry the onion for about 3 minutes, or until soft. Add the garlic, ginger and spices. Stir for another minute.

3 Add the lentils and 500 ml (17 fl oz/2 cups) water and bring to the boil. Lower the heat and simmer, stirring occasionally, for 15 minutes, or until all the water has been absorbed. Watch carefully towards the end of cooking time, as the mixture could burn on the bottom of the pan.

4 Transfer to a serving bowl and serve warm or at room temperature with pitta toasts or with naan or pitta bread for older babies and puréed to a smoother texture for younger babies.

pitta toasts Preheat the oven to 180°C (350°F/Gas 4). Cut 4 rounds of pitta bread into wedges and brush lightly with oil. Arrange on a baking tray and cook for 5–7 minutes, or until lightly browned and crisp.

The foundations of healthy eating are now laid. By making vegetables a regular part of your baby's menu, you will guarantee that they are enjoyed in the future.

Vegetable casserole

1 tablespoon olive oil

½ brown onion, finely chopped

1 garlic clove, crushed (optional)

½ celery stalk, finely diced

½ carrot, diced

50 g (1¾ oz/¼ cup) brown lentils

200 g (7 oz) tin diced tomatoes

185 ml (6 fl oz/¾ cup) salt-reduced vegetable or chicken stock

150 g (5½ oz) pumpkin (winter squash), deseeded and cut into 1 cm (½ inch) cubes

½ zucchini (courgette), quartered lengthways and cut into 1 cm (½ inch) slices

1 Preheat the oven to 200°C (400°F/Gas 6).

2 Heat the oil in a flameproof casserole dish over medium heat. Add the onion, garlic, celery and carrot and cook for 5 minutes, or until softened. Add the lentils, tomato and stock and stir to combine. Cover and bake for 40 minutes. Add the pumpkin and zucchini and cook for a further 10–12 minutes, or until tender.

3 Mash lightly with a fork or purée to serve to younger babies if necessary.

Prep time 15 minutes

Cooking time 1 hour

Makes 3–4 serves

Jelly (gelatine dessert) is a tasty textural delight for toddlers. This recipe is also a vitamin- and fibre-packed alternative to ready-made varieties.

Fruit jelly

1 tablespoon gelatine powder

375 ml (13 fl oz/1½ cups) unsweetened fruit juice

200 g (7 oz/¾ cup) puréed fresh or drained tin fruit in natural juice

Prep time 10 minutes

Cooking time 5 minutes

Makes 6 serves

1 Sprinkle the gelatine over 125 ml (4 fl oz/½ cup) cool water in a small saucepan. Heat through, then add the fruit juice and heat through again. Pour into a mixing bowl and leave until it begins to thicken. Stir in the puréed fruit until well combined.

2 Transfer to small dishes and refrigerate until set.

Good rice pudding takes time. Make this recipe as a special dessert for the whole family. Add sultanas (golden raisins) to boost its fibre and give it bursts of sweet flavour.

Rice pudding

110 g (3¾ oz/½ cup) arborio rice

1 litre (35 fl oz/4 cups) milk

2 tablespoons caster (superfine) sugar

1 teaspoon natural vanilla extract

1 teaspoon unsalted butter (optional)

pinch of ground cinnamon (optional)

fresh berries, to garnish (optional)

1 Preheat the oven to 180°C (350°F/Gas 4).

2 Place the rice, milk, sugar, vanilla and butter and cinnamon, if using, in a baking dish and stir.

3 Bake for about 1½ hours, stirring every 15 minutes to make sure it doesn't stick to the dish. Remove the pudding from the oven when it has the consistency of creamed rice. Do not overcook or it may dry out. Cool slightly and top with fresh berries.

Prep time 10 minutes

Cooking time 1½ hours

Makes 4 serves

Toddler food

A wholegrain cereal like oats is rich in energy-giving carbohydrates, essential fats and minerals. Team it with banana and it becomes a great source of B vitamins, including folate, as well as vitamin C and potassium.

Banana porridge

1 tablespoon quick-cook oats

1 tablespoon cold water

1½ tablespoons hot water

2 teaspoons mashed banana

milk or cooled boiled water

Prep time 5 minutes

Cooking time 2 minutes

Serves 1

1 Combine the quick-cook oats with the cold water in a small saucepan. Add the hot water and bring to the boil, stirring. Reduce the heat and simmer for 30 seconds or until the mixture is thick and creamy.

2 Remove the porridge from the heat and stir through the mashed banana. Mix with enough milk or cooled boiled water to produce the required consistency.

While adult commercial cereals can be used for a toddler's breakfast, some are high in sugar and salt. This muesli (granola) has all the goodness of whole grains and dried fruits without any unwanted extras.

Home-made muesli

150 g (5½ oz/1½ cups) rolled (porridge) oats

2 tablespoons wheatgerm

30 g (1 oz/¼ cup) raw oatmeal

20 g (¾ oz/¼ cup) processed wheat bran

60 g (2¼ oz/½ cup) sultanas (golden raisins)

30 g (1 oz/⅓ cup) dried apple, chopped

90 g (3¼ oz/½ cup) dried apricots, chopped

Prep time 10 minutes

Cooking time Nil

Serves 8

1 Combine all the ingredients together and store in an airtight container for up to 4 weeks. To serve, pour over a little milk, place in a saucepan and stir over medium heat for 30–60 seconds to soften; or place in a microwave for 20–30 seconds.

2 Alternatively, blend the dry muesli in a food processor until almost fine. Serve with other dried fruits, fresh fruit, yoghurt or a drizzle of honey (only for children over 12 months) or fruit purée.

The ultimate in convenience food, eggs make a perfect meal at any time of the day for a growing toddler. Don't just save them for breakfast!

Fluffy omelette

1 egg yolk
2 egg whites
1 teaspoon olive oil or margarine

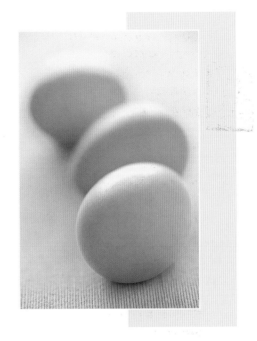

1 Lightly beat the egg yolk with 1 teaspoon water. Beat the egg whites to soft peaks and stir in the yolk mixture.

2 Heat the oil or margarine in a small frying pan and pour in the egg mixture. Cook quickly on one side, then turn and cook until just firm.

variations Fillings of flaked fish, such as red salmon, finely chopped sautéed zucchini (courgette) and onion, mushrooms, tomato or grated cheddar cheese can be used. Place along the centre of the omelette on the uncooked side, then fold over to enclose the filling. Cook until the omelette is cooked through, turning once.

Prep time 5 minutes
Cooking time 5 minutes
Serves 1

Bread is an important staple food for the growing toddler. Vary the types of bread you use for this recipe; try wholegrain, rye or even fruit bread.

French toast

1 egg, lightly beaten

2 teaspoons milk

margarine or oil, for frying

2 thick slices wholemeal (whole-wheat) bread

4 strawberries, sliced

2 teaspoons honey or maple syrup

Prep time 5 minutes

Cooking time 2 minutes

Serves 1–2

1 Combine the egg and milk in a bowl large enough to fit the bread, and beat lightly with a fork.

2 Heat the margarine or oil in a frying pan over medium heat. Dip the bread into the egg mixture, drain off the excess, then cook until golden brown on both sides. Remove to a plate, top with the strawberries and drizzle with honey or maple syrup.

hint If desired, cut the bread into different shapes using biscuit cutters; however, you will need to increase the bread to four slices to allow for wastage.

Research shows that a healthy diet is encouraged when children eat with their family regularly. Enjoy this recipe with your toddler as a special breakfast.

Eggs en cocotte

½ teaspoon olive oil

4 eggs

2 tablespoons snipped chives

4 slices thick wholegrain (whole-wheat) bread

15 g (½ oz) margarine

Tomato sauce

1 tablespoon olive oil

1 garlic clove, crushed

3 vine-ripened tomatoes (about 300 g/10½ oz), peeled, seeded and chopped

Prep time 15 minutes

Cooking time 30 minutes

Serves 4

1 Preheat the oven to 180°C (350°F/Gas 4). To make the tomato sauce, heat the oil in a heavy-based frying pan. Add the garlic and cook for 30 seconds. Add the tomato and season with salt and freshly ground black pepper. Cook over medium heat for 15 minutes, or until thickened.

2 Grease four 125 ml (4 fl oz/½ cup) ramekins with the olive oil, then carefully break 1 egg into each, trying not to break the yolk. Pour the tomato sauce evenly around the outside of each egg, so the yolk is still visible. Sprinkle with chives and season lightly with salt and freshly ground black pepper.

3 Place the ramekins in a deep baking dish and pour in enough hot water to come halfway up the outside of the ramekins. Bake for about 10–12 minutes, or until the egg white is set.

4 Toast the bread and lightly spread the slices with the margarine, then cut into thick fingers. Serve immediately with the cooked eggs.

Soya beans are the perfect size for tiny fingers to practise their fine motor skills. They also provide vitamins, high-quality protein, iron and zinc.

Home-made baked beans

550 g (1 lb 4 oz/3 cups) dried soya beans

400 g (14 oz) tin diced tomatoes

250 ml (9 fl oz/1 cup) salt-reduced vegetable stock

1 bay leaf

2 tablespoons chopped parsley

pinch of dried thyme

1 tablespoon vegetable oil

Prep time 5 minutes

Cooking time 4 hours 40 minutes

Serves 4

1 Cook the soya beans in plenty of water for about 4 hours, or until tender. Drain. Preheat the oven to 180°C (350°F/Gas 4).

2 Put the soya beans in a casserole dish and add the tomato, stock, herbs and oil. Bake, covered, for 40 minutes.

hints If you want a thicker consistency, remove the lid of the casserole dish and cook for a further 10–15 minutes, or until reduced to the desired consistency. Instead of using dried soya beans, you can use the same amount of drained, tin soya beans.

A source of vitamins A, C and the B group, blueberries make these pancakes a much healthier breakfast for toddlers than pancakes with maple syrup.

Blueberry pancakes

250 g (9 oz/2 cups) plain
(all-purpose) flour

2 teaspoons baking powder

1 teaspoon bicarbonate of soda
(baking soda)

90 g (3¼ oz/⅓ cup) sugar

2 eggs

80 g (2¾ oz) margarine, melted, plus
extra for frying

310 ml (10¾ fl oz/1¼ cups) milk

310 g (11 oz/2 cups) blueberries,
fresh or frozen (see hint)

Prep time 10–15 minutes
Cooking time 18 minutes
Makes 6

1 Sift the flour, baking powder and bicarbonate of soda into a large bowl. Add the sugar and make a well in the centre. Using a fork, whisk the eggs, melted margarine and milk together in a bowl and add to the dry ingredients, stirring just to combine (add more milk if you prefer a thinner batter). Gently fold in the blueberries.

2 Heat a frying pan and brush lightly with extra melted margarine or oil. Pour 125 ml (4 fl oz/½ cup) batter into the pan and spread out to make a pancake about 15 cm (6 inches) in diameter. Cook over low heat until bubbles appear and pop on the surface.

3 Turn the pancake over and cook the other side (these pancakes can be difficult to handle so take care when turning). Transfer to a plate and cover to keep warm while cooking the remaining batter. The pancakes are delicious served warm with blueberry coulis (see recipe below) and Greek-style plain yoghurt.

hint If you use frozen blueberries, there is no need to thaw them.

blueberry coulis Put 310 g (11 oz/2 cups) fresh or frozen blueberries in a blender or food processor and blend until puréed. Strain through a fine sieve to remove skin and make a smooth sauce. Stir in 2 teaspoons icing (confectioners') sugar. Stir the coulis through plain yoghurt or serve plain with pancakes, ice cream, fruit salad or breakfast cereal. Store any left-over coulis in the refrigerator for up to 3 days.

This creamy, cheesy pasta meal always seems to be a firm favourite with toddlers. And the dairy it contains is good for young children; it is rich in calcium, which is needed for growing teeth and bones.

Macaroni cheese

30 g (1 oz) margarine

1 tablespoon plain (all-purpose) flour

250 ml (9 fl oz/1 cup) milk

60 g (2¼ oz/½ cup) grated cheddar cheese

350 g (12 oz/2¼ cups) macaroni, cooked

1 tomato, cut into wedges

1 Melt the butter in a small saucepan. Blend in the flour and cook for 1 minute.

2 Remove the pan from the heat and gradually blend in the milk. Return to the heat and cook, stirring, until the sauce boils and thickens.

3 Reduce the heat and simmer for 3 minutes. Add the grated cheese and stir until melted. Mix the macaroni through the sauce and season with freshly ground black pepper to taste. Serve with the tomato wedges.

Prep time 5 minutes

Cooking time 10 minutes

Serves 4

These tasty cakes make a great meal or even a nutritious snack served cold. They are packed with energy-giving carbohydrates, as well as vitamins, minerals (especially calcium, if you mash in the bones) and healthy fats.

Salmon & basil fish cakes

2 medium all-purpose potatoes, quartered

415 g (14¾ oz) tin pink salmon, drained, skin and large bones removed

½ teaspoon grated lime zest

4 spring onions (scallions), finely chopped

1 handful basil leaves, roughly chopped

1 tablespoon capers, rinsed, drained and roughly chopped

1 egg yolk

1 egg, lightly beaten

1 tablespoon milk

40 g (1½ oz/⅓ cup) plain (all-purpose) flour

70 g (2½ oz/¾ cup) dry breadcrumbs

oil, for shallow-frying

Prep time 20 minutes +
  30 minutes refrigeration
Cooking time 20 minutes
Makes 8

1 Cook the potatoes in a large saucepan of boiling water until just tender. Drain and lightly mash, leaving some large pieces. Allow the potatoes to cool.

2 Meanwhile, in a bowl, gently flake the salmon into large pieces. Add the lime zest, spring onion, basil, capers and egg yolk. Mix lightly then stir in the mashed potato. Season with freshly ground black pepper.

3 Combine the egg and milk in a shallow bowl. Spread the flour and breadcrumbs out on separate plates. With wet hands, shape the salmon mixture into eight patties about 6 cm (2½ inches) in diameter, pressing the mixture firmly together. Dust with flour, and shake off any excess. Dip the fish cakes into the egg mixture, then coat in the breadcrumbs. Place the patties on a tray and refrigerate, covered, for 30 minutes, or until firm.

4 Add enough oil to come one-third of the way up a large, deep frying pan. Heat over high heat. Cook the patties for 3–4 minutes each side, or until golden and heated through. Drain on paper towels. Serve with mashed sweet potato and minted peas.

hints The patties can be made several hours ahead and refrigerated. You can substitute tin tuna for salmon if desired.

Fruit-based breakfasts are rich in vitamins, minerals and fibre, and are a quick and yummy way for kids to start the day. If berries aren't in season, use a medley of whatever happens to be ripe and tasty in your fruit bowl.

Mixed berry couscous

185 g (6½ oz/1 cup) instant couscous

500 ml (17 fl oz/2 cups) apple and cranberry juice

1 cinnamon stick

250 g (9 oz/2 cups) frozen raspberries, thawed

250 g (9 oz/1⅔ cups) frozen blueberries, thawed

2 teaspoons orange zest, plus extra, to garnish

250 g (9 oz/1⅔ cups) strawberries, halved

185 g (6½ oz/¾ cup) Greek-style plain yoghurt

fresh mint leaves, to garnish

1 Put the instant couscous in a bowl. Pour the apple and cranberry juice into a saucepan and add the cinnamon stick. Cover and bring to the boil, then remove from the heat and pour over the couscous. Cover the couscous with plastic wrap and leave for about 5 minutes, or until all the liquid has been absorbed. After this time, remove the cinnamon stick from the bowl.

2 Gently pat the thawed berries with paper towels to absorb the excess juices. Separate the grains of couscous with a fork, then gently fold in the orange zest and most of the berries. Spoon the couscous mixture into four serving bowls and sprinkle with the remaining berries. Serve with a generous dollop of the yoghurt. Garnish with mint leaves and orange zest and serve.

Prep time 15 minutes

Cooking time 5 minutes

Serves 4

This recipe needs only to be assembled and heated—making it perfect for hungry toddlers. It is also filled with protein, energy-giving carbohydrates and the B vitamin niacin.

Creamy chicken & corn soup

1 litre (35 fl oz/4 cups) salt-reduced chicken stock

40 g (1½ oz/½ cup) small pasta

175 g (6 oz/1 cup) finely chopped cooked chicken (see hint)

125 g (4½ oz/½ cup) tin creamed corn

1 tablespoon chopped parsley

Prep time 10 minutes

Cooking time 20 minutes

Serves 6

1 Put the stock and pasta in a saucepan. Bring to the boil, then reduce the heat and simmer for 10–12 minutes, or until the pasta is very tender. Add the chicken and corn and simmer for 5 minutes.

2 Stir in the parsley and cool slightly. Process in a blender or food processor until smooth. Reheat to serve or refrigerate in an airtight container for up to 3 days, or freeze in portion sizes.

hint For the cooked chicken, use skinless barbecued (grilled) chicken. Alternatively, use chopped boneless, skinless, raw chicken breast and add to the stock with the pasta.

These pizzas are a quick lunch that your toddler can help you prepare. Let them spread on the tomato sauce or sprinkle over the cheese. This will make the pizzas an even more anticipated meal.

Instant mini pizzas

3 English muffins, split in half

margarine or olive oil

3 tablespoons chunky tomato-based pasta sauce

90 g (3¼ oz) cooked ham, bacon or chicken, cut into strips

60 g (2¼ oz/½ cup) grated cheddar cheese

Prep time 5 minutes

Cooking time 10 minutes

Makes 6

1 Preheat the oven to 240°C (475°F/Gas 8).

2 Lightly spread the muffin halves with margarine or olive oil. Spread the tomato-based pasta sauce over the muffins, top with the strips of ham and cover with the cheese.

3 Place onto a baking tray and bake for 8–10 minutes, or until the muffins are crisp and the cheese has melted and turned golden.

variations Adult and older children's servings can be garnished with pineapple pieces, avocado chunks or olives before heating in the oven. Small-sized pitta bread (pockets) can be used instead of muffins.

This recipe is a great way to serve up potatoes—a little known source of vitamin C. It makes a great picnic food that can be served cold and cut it into bite-sized pieces for little ones or larger wedges for grown-ups.

Spanish omelette

1 kg (2 lb 4 oz) all-purpose potatoes

2 large red (Spanish) onions, coarsely chopped

50 g (1¾ oz) unsalted butter

2 tablespoons olive oil

1 garlic clove, crushed

2 tablespoons finely chopped parsley

4 eggs, lightly beaten

Prep time 20 minutes
Cooking time 35 minutes
Serves 4–6

1 Cut the potatoes into small cubes and place in a large ovenproof saucepan. Cover with water, then bring to the boil and cook, uncovered, for 3 minutes. Remove the pan from the heat and allow to stand, covered, for 8 minutes, or until the potato is just tender. Drain well.

2 Heat the butter and oil in a deep, non-stick frying pan over medium heat. Add the onions and garlic and cook for 8 minutes, stirring occasionally. Add the potato and cook for another 5 minutes. Remove the vegetables with a slotted spoon and transfer them to a large bowl, reserving the oil in the frying pan. Add the parsley and eggs to the potato and onion and mix until well combined.

3 Reheat the oil in the frying pan over high heat and add the mixture. Reduce the heat to low and cook, covered, for about 10 minutes, or until the underside of the omelette is golden. Brown the top of the omelette under a hot grill (broiler).

As with Spanish omelette, this recipe can also be served cold as part of a picnic. Try serving these fritters with your toddler's favourite dipping sauce and see how much they enjoy these vegies!

Corn & capsicum fritters

1 large red capsicum (pepper)

2–3 cobs fresh corn kernels (about 300 g/10½ oz) or 400 g (14 oz) tin corn kernels, drained

oil, for frying

2 tablespoons chopped parsley, coriander (cilantro) leaves, chives or dill

3 eggs

Prep time 20 minutes

Cooking time 10 minutes

Serves 4

1 Cut the capsicum into large pieces, discarding the seeds and membrane, then chop into small pieces. Cut the kernels from the fresh corn using a sharp knife. Heat 2 tablespoons oil in a frying pan. Add the corn and stir over medium heat for 2 minutes. Add the capsicum and stir for another 2 minutes. Transfer the vegetables to a bowl. Add the herbs and stir well to combine. Beat the eggs in a small bowl with a little freshly ground black pepper. Stir the egg gradually into the vegetable mixture.

2 Heat a non-stick frying pan over medium heat. Add enough oil to cover the base. Drop large spoonfuls of the vegetable mixture into the oil, a few at a time. Cook the fritters for 1–2 minutes, or until brown. Turn and cook the other side. Drain on paper towels and keep warm while you cook the remainder.

hints These fritters may be served with sour cream and a green salad for lunch, or as an accompaniment to a main course. Take care as these fritters contain no flour, so they cook quickly. You want them to still be a little creamy in the middle when done.

Soup is a great way to get vegetables into toddlers. Make sure it is cool enough to eat and then let them dunk toast fingers for a nourishing 'hands on' meal.

Tomato soup

20 g (¾ oz) margarine or 1 tablespoon olive oil

1 celery stalk, finely chopped

1 brown onion, finely chopped

1 carrot, finely chopped

1 garlic clove, crushed

700 g (1 lb 9 oz) tomato-based pasta sauce

750 ml (26 fl oz/3 cups) salt-reduced chicken or vegetable stock

1 teaspoon sugar

1 parsley sprig

1 bay leaf

250 ml (9 fl oz/1 cup) milk

2 teaspoons chopped parsley (optional)

wholegrain (whole-wheat) toast, to serve

1 Heat the margarine or oil in a saucepan and sauté the celery, onion and carrot for 3–4 minutes. Add the garlic and cook for 30 seconds. Add the pasta sauce, chicken or vegetable stock, sugar, parsley sprig and bay leaf. Bring to the boil, then simmer for 10 minutes. Remove the parsley and bay leaf.

2 Purée the soup in a blender, then return it to the pan. Stir through the milk and cook until hot.

3 Garnish with the parsley, if desired, and serve with toast.

Prep time 10 minutes

Cooking time 20 minutes

Serves 4

Toddlers can be too tired to eat at night, so make lunch the main meal of the day. This protein- and carbohydrate-rich pasta meal makes for a perfect lunchtime sandwich substitute.

Tomato, tuna & white bean pasta

25 g (1 oz/¼ cup) small shell pasta or other small pasta

90 g (3¼ oz/⅓ cup) chunky tomato-based pasta sauce

95 g (3¼ oz) tin tuna in spring water, drained

2 tablespoons drained, rinsed tin cannellini beans

1 teaspoon chopped drained, rinsed capers in brine

1 teaspoon finely chopped fresh basil

1 Cook the pasta in a saucepan of boiling water until *al dente*. Drain and keep warm.

2 Meanwhile, put the pasta sauce, tuna, beans, capers and basil in a small saucepan and stir over medium heat for 1–2 minutes, or until heated through. Toss through the pasta to serve.

Prep time 5 minutes

Cooking time 10 minutes

Serves 2

This is a great way of turning leftovers into a tasty and nutritious meal rich in vitamins A, C and the B group, as well as potassium.

Bubble & squeak

150 g (5½ oz/1 cup) cooked all-purpose potato

150 g (5½ oz/1 cup) cooked pumpkin (winter squash)

50 g (1¾ oz/1 cup) grated cabbage, cooked

50 g (1¾ oz/1 cup) small broccoli florets, cooked

4 eggs, beaten

2 chives, snipped

20 g (¾ oz) margarine or 1 tablespoon olive oil

1 Put the vegetables in a bowl and mix well with the egg and chives.

2 Heat the margarine or oil in a large frying pan and add the vegetable mixture. Cook over medium heat until the underside is golden, then cut into quarters and turn. Cook the mixture for a little longer until the surface is golden and the egg set. Alternatively, once the underside is cooked, put the frying pan under a hot grill (broiler) for 1–2 minutes, or until the top is set.

hints Any combination of left-over cooked vegetables can be used. Left-over cooked meat can also be chopped and added to the mixture.

Prep time 10 minutes

Cooking time 5 minutes

Serves 4

Kidney beans, vegetables and pasta combine to make this a hearty and nutritious meal for the whole family. Prepare this recipe ahead of time and keep it in the fridge for warming winter meals through the week or on weekends.

Minestrone

2 tablespoons olive oil

1 brown onion, chopped

1 slice rindless bacon, finely chopped

3 carrots, halved lengthways and chopped

3 zucchini (courgettes), halved lengthways and chopped

2 celery stalks, sliced

2 all-purpose potatoes, chopped

400 g (14 oz) tin diced tomatoes

400 g (14 oz) tin 4-bean mix, drained and rinsed

30 g (1 oz/⅓ cup) small pasta shapes

125 g (4½ oz/1 cup) green beans, trimmed and sliced

grated parmesan cheese

chopped parsley

1 Heat the oil in a large saucepan and sauté the onion and bacon until the onion is soft. Add the carrot, zucchini, celery, potatoes, tomatoes and 4-bean mix and cook, stirring, for 1 minute.

2 Add 2.5 litres (87 fl oz/10 cups) water to the pan and season with freshly ground black pepper. Bring to the boil, then reduce the heat and simmer, covered, for 1 hour.

3 Stir in the pasta and green beans and simmer for 12 minutes, or until tender. Sprinkle the minestrone with parmesan cheese and chopped parsley and serve with crusty bread.

Prep time 15 minutes

Cooking time 1 hour 20 minutes

Serves 20

Children like what they know, so if they only ever get to know white bread, that is all they will ever want. Expose them early on to a wide range of breads. Rye, wholemeal (whole-wheat), wholegrain and pitta pockets are all good bread choices.

Tuna, caper & bean sandwich

95 g (3¼ oz) tin tuna in spring water, drained

1 teaspoon finely chopped drained, rinsed capers in brine

3 teaspoons whole-egg mayonnaise

2 teaspoons tin cannellini beans, mashed

bread of your choice

1 Put the tuna, capers, mayonnaise and cannellini beans in a bowl and mix well.

2 Add to the bread of your choice.

Prep time 5 minutes

Cooking time Nil

Serves 1

Dried red lentils are excellent as they are the quickest legume to cook. Legumes are a good source of protein, vitamins, minerals and fibre.

Crispy lentil balls

125 g (4½ oz/½ cup) red lentils

2 bulb spring onions (scallions), chopped

1 garlic clove, crushed

½ teaspoon ground cumin

40 g (1½ oz/½ cup) fresh breadcrumbs

60 g (2¼ oz/½ cup) grated cheddar cheese

½ large zucchini (courgette), grated

70 g (2½ oz/½ cup) polenta

oil, for deep-frying

Prep time 20 minutes

Cooking time 15 minutes

Makes 15

1 Put the lentils in a saucepan and cover with water. Bring to the boil, reduce the heat to low, then cover and simmer for 10 minutes, or until the lentils are tender. Drain and rinse well under cold water.

2 Combine half the lentils in a food processor or blender with the spring onions and garlic. Process for 10 seconds, or until the mixture is pulpy. Transfer to a large bowl and add the remaining lentils, cumin, breadcrumbs, cheese and zucchini. Stir until combined.

3 Using your hands, roll level tablespoons of the mixture into balls and toss lightly in the polenta.

4 Heat the oil in a heavy-based pan. Gently lower half the balls into medium–hot oil. Cook for 1 minute, or until golden brown and crisp. Carefully remove from the oil with tongs or a slotted spoon and drain on paper towels. Repeat the process with the remaining balls. Serve hot with your favourite dipping sauce.

This frittata combines vegetables with a nourishing cheese and egg base, which is a great— if slightly sneaky—way of upping your toddler's vegetable intake.

Leek, zucchini & cheese frittata

2 tablespoons olive oil

3 leeks, thinly sliced (white part only)

2 zucchini (courgettes), cut into matchstick pieces

1 garlic clove, crushed

5 eggs, lightly beaten

4 tablespoons freshly grated parmesan cheese

4 tablespoons diced Swiss cheese

Prep time 20 minutes

Cooking time 40 minutes

Serves 4

1   Heat 1 tablespoon of the olive oil in small ovenproof pan. Add the leek and cook, stirring, over low heat until slightly softened. Cover and cook the leek for 10 minutes, stirring occasionally. Add the zucchini and garlic and cook for another 10 minutes. Transfer the mixture to a bowl. Allow to cool, then season with freshly ground black pepper. Add the egg and cheeses and stir through.

2   Heat the remaining oil in the pan, then add the egg mixture and smooth the surface. Cook over low heat for 15 minutes, or until the frittata is almost set.

3   Put the pan under a preheated hot grill (broiler) for 3–5 minutes, or until the top is set and golden. Allow the frittata to stand for 5 minutes before cutting into wedges and serving. Serve with a fresh green salad.

Most of us eat far too much salt, even young children. When preparing this dish, use salt-reduced or no-added-salt tin tomatoes, tomato paste and stock.

Simple bolognese

2 tablespoons olive oil

1 brown onion, finely chopped

1 garlic clove, crushed

500 g (1 lb 2 oz) minced (ground) beef

25 g (1 oz/¼ cup) chopped mushrooms

2 tablespoons tomato paste (concentrated purée)

400 g (14 oz) tin chopped tomatoes

125 ml (4 fl oz/½ cup) salt-reduced beef stock or water

1 tablespoon chopped parsley

cooked pasta of your choice

parmesan or cheddar cheese, grated (optional)

1 Heat the oil in a heavy-based saucepan and sauté the onion and garlic until tender. Add the beef and brown well, breaking the meat up with a spoon as it cooks.

2 Add the chopped mushrooms to the saucepan and cook for 1 minute. Blend in the tomato paste.

3 Stir in the tomato, stock or water, parsley and season with freshly ground black pepper. Bring to the boil and then reduce the heat and simmer, stirring occasionally, for 20 minutes.

4 Toss the sauce through hot, drained pasta, such as spaghetti or linguine. Sprinkle with grated parmesan or cheddar cheese, if desired, and serve with a crisp green salad.

5 You can freeze the left-over sauce in portion sizes for up to 3 months.

Prep time 10 minutes
Cooking time 30 minutes
Serves 8

The lean minced (ground) beef used in this recipe is not only easy for toddlers to chew, but it will make a significant contribution to your toddler's iron intake.

Mini shepherd's pies

1 tablespoon oil

500 g (1 lb 2 oz) minced (ground) beef

2 tablespoons plain (all-purpose) flour

250 ml (9 fl oz/1 cup) salt-reduced beef stock

2 tablespoons chopped parsley

4 all-purpose potatoes, cooked

60 ml (2 fl oz/¼ cup) milk

15 g (½ oz) margarine

270 g (9½ oz/2 cups) frozen mixed vegetables (peas, beans, carrots), thawed

60 g (2¼ oz/½ cup) grated cheddar cheese

25 g (1 oz/¼ cup) dried breadcrumbs

1　Preheat the oven to 180°C (350°F/Gas 4). Heat the oil in a frying pan, add the meat and brown, breaking the meat up with a spoon as it cooks. Stir in the flour and cook, stirring, for 1 minute.

2　Blend in the stock, parsley and some freshly ground black pepper to taste. Simmer, stirring, for about 5 minutes, or until the mixture thickens.

3　Mash the potatoes well and beat until smooth with the milk and margarine, adding more of each if needed.

4　Spoon the meat mixture into four small ramekin dishes. Top with an even amount of the mixed vegetables and spread the mashed potato over the top.

5　Mix together the cheese and breadcrumbs and sprinkle over each pie. Bake in the oven for 10–15 minutes, or until the tops are golden.

Prep time 10 minutes

Cooking time 30 minutes

Makes 4

This recipe can be reinvented many times over by using various combinations of vegetables and tuna, or other diced meats, plus any one of a variety of fun pasta shapes.

Quick pasta with tomato sauce

1 tablespoon extra virgin olive oil

1 garlic clove, crushed

400 g (14 oz) tin diced Roma (plum) tomatoes

250 g (9 oz/2¾ cups) penne or farfalle (bow-tie) pasta

1 tablespoon shaved parmesan cheese (optional)

Prep time 5 minutes
Cooking time 10 minutes
Serves 4

1 Heat the olive oil in a frying pan over medium heat. Cook the garlic, stirring constantly, for 30 seconds. Add the tomatoes and stir through. Reduce the heat to low and cook for a further 8–10 minutes, stirring occasionally, or until reduced.

2 Meanwhile, cook the pasta in a large saucepan of salted boiling water until al dente. Drain and return to the saucepan.

3 Add the cooked tomatoes to the pasta and stir through.

4 Spoon a small portion into a bowl and sprinkle with parmesan cheese, if desired.

variation Stir through the tomato sauce a spoonful of mashed, drained tin tuna (preferably in spring water, not oil or brine) and just cooked (not mushy) vegetables such as diced zucchini (courgettes), diced carrot, diced butternut pumpkin (squash), finely chopped English spinach and finely chopped flat-leaf (Italian) parsley.

Protein is an important part of a growing child's diet. Main meals for vegetarian children should always include a vegetable protein, such as tofu.

Vegetable & noodle stir-fry

50 g (1¾ oz) cellophane or egg noodles

2 teaspoons oil

1 carrot, chopped

1 celery stalk, chopped

1 small zucchini (courgette), halved lenthways, sliced

½ red capsicum (pepper), deseeded, chopped

60 g (2¼ oz/½ cup) cauliflower florets

30 g (1 oz/½ cup) broccoli florets

30 g (1 oz/¼ cup) sliced green beans

½ garlic clove, crushed

2 teaspoons salt-reduced soy sauce

1 Place the noodles in a bowl. Cover with boiling water. Leave to stand for 1 minute, or until tender. Drain.

2 Heat the oil in a wok or frying pan. Add the carrot, celery, zucchini, capsicum, cauliflower, broccoli, beans and garlic and stir-fry for 4–5 minutes.

3 Toss the noodles through the vegetables with the soy sauce. Stir-fry for 1 minute. Serve immediately.

variation To make this a more substantial meal, cut 200 g (7 oz) silken firm tofu into 2 cm (¾ inch) cubes or grate 200 g (7 oz) hard tofu and add to the stir-fry after cooking the vegetables. Gently toss through for 1 minute to heat through. If adding tofu, reduce the amount of vegetables.

Prep time 10 minutes

Cooking time 7 minutes

Serves 4

Using frozen foods won't compromise your family's nutrition. That's because their cooking and freezing are so quick that loss of important nutrients is small, which means more vitamins for everyone.

Fried rice

2 tablespoons peanut oil

2 eggs, well beaten

4 slices rindless bacon, chopped

2 teaspoons finely grated fresh
   ginger

1 garlic clove, crushed

6 spring onions (scallions),
   finely chopped

50 g (1¾ oz) red capsicum (pepper),
   deseeded and diced

1 teaspoon sesame oil

750 g (1 lb 10 oz/4 cups) cooked,
   cold, long-grain white rice
   (see hint)

100 g (3½ oz/⅔ cup) frozen peas,
   thawed

100 g (3½ oz) cooked, chopped
   chicken

2 tablespoons salt-reduced soy sauce

1 Heat a large heavy-based wok until very hot, add about 2 teaspoons of the peanut oil and swirl. Pour in the eggs and swirl to coat the side of the wok. Cook until just set. Remove from the wok, roll up and set aside. Add the remaining oil to the wok and stir-fry the bacon for 2 minutes. Add the ginger, garlic, spring onion and capsicum and stir-fry for 2 minutes.

2 Add the sesame oil and the rice. Stir-fry, tossing regularly, until the rice is heated through.

3 Cut the egg into thin strips and add to the wok with the peas and the chicken. Cover and steam for 1 minute, or until everything is heated through. Stir in the soy sauce and serve.

hint White rice almost triples in bulk during cooking, so you will need about 250 g (9 oz/1¼ cups) uncooked rice to give 750 g (1 lb 10 oz/4 cups) cooked rice. Alternatively, you can buy pre-cooked frozen rice. Ensure it is thawed before using it in this recipe.

Prep time 25 minutes

Cooking time 10 minutes

Serves 4

Make this an interactive meal and let your toddler assemble the enchiladas.
Don't forget to relax about the mess!

Bean enchiladas

1 tablespoon light olive oil

1 brown onion, thinly sliced

3 garlic cloves, crushed

2 teaspoons ground cumin

125 ml (4 fl oz/½ cup) salt-reduced
    vegetable stock

3 tomatoes, peeled, deseeded and
    chopped

1 tablespoon tomato paste
    (concentrated purée)

800 g (14 oz) tin 3-bean mix

2 tablespoons chopped coriander
    (cilantro) leaves

8 flour tortillas

1 small avocado, chopped

125 g (4½ oz/½ cup) light sour
    cream

1 handful coriander (cilantro) sprigs

115 g (4 oz/2 cups) shredded lettuce

Prep time 20 minutes

Cooking time 25 minutes

Makes 8

1 Preheat the oven to 170°C (325°F/Gas 3).

2 Heat the oil in a deep frying pan over medium heat. Add
the onion and cook for 3–4 minutes, or until just soft.
Add the garlic and cook for a further 30 seconds. Add the
cumin, vegetable stock, tomato and tomato paste and
cook for 6–8 minutes, or until the mixture is quite thick
and pulpy. Season with freshly ground black pepper.

3 Drain and rinse the 3-bean mix. Add the beans to the
sauce and cook for 5 minutes to heat through, then add
the chopped coriander.

4 Meanwhile, wrap the tortillas in foil and warm in the
oven for 3–4 minutes.

5 Place a tortilla on a plate and spread with a large scoop
of the bean mixture. Top with some avocado, sour
cream, coriander sprigs and lettuce. Roll the enchiladas
up, tucking in the ends. Cut each one in half to serve.

variations For beef enchiladas, use only half the
quantity of 3-bean mix and add 500 g (1 lb 2 oz) lean
minced (ground) beef. Cook the beef with the garlic
for 5–6 minutes, or until browned and cooked through,
breaking up any lumps with the back of a spoon.
Alternatively, for tuna enchiladas, use only half the
quantity of 3-bean mix and add 425 g (15 oz) tin tuna
in brine, drained. Add the tuna with the stock.

Iodine is an essential nutrient for humans, both large and small; fish and seafood are excellent sources.

Chinese-style fish on vegetables

1 carrot, cut into 5 cm (2 inch) matchstick strips

½ celery stalk, cut into 5 cm (2 inch) matchstick strips

2 small spring onions (scallions), cut into 5 cm (2 inch) matchstick strips

4 mushrooms, cut into matchstick strips

4 boneless white fish fillets (about 400 g/14 oz), skin on

2 teaspoons salt-reduced soy sauce

2 teaspoons vegetable oil

1 Put the vegetable strips on a dish that will fit in a steamer. Arrange the fish, skin side up, on the vegetables. Combine the soy sauce and vegetable oil together, then pour over the fish. Place the dish in a steamer, cover, and steam over simmering water for about 10 minutes, or until the fish flakes when tested with a fork.

hint To cook this dish in the oven, arrange the ingredients, as above, on a rack in an ovenproof dish and add 60–125 ml (2–4 fl oz/¼–½ cup) water. Cover and bake in a preheated 180°C (350°F/Gas 4) oven or 15 minutes, or until the fish flakes easily and is cooked through.

Prep time 10 minutes
Cooking time 10 minutes
Serves 4

Stroganoff is a hearty and tasty winter meal that is a good source of protein and the minerals iron and zinc.

Beef stroganoff

500 g (1 lb 2 oz) lean rump steak

2 tablespoons plain (all-purpose) flour

2 tablespoons olive oil

1 large brown onion, sliced

1 garlic clove, crushed

150 g (5½ oz) mushrooms, sliced

185 ml (6 fl oz/¾ cup) salt-reduced beef stock

1 tablespoon tomato paste (concentrated purée)

185 g (6½ oz/¾ cup) sour cream

1 tablespoon finely chopped flat-leaf (Italian) parsley

Prep time 15 minutes

Cooking time 15 minutes

Serves 4

1   Cut the beef into strips. Place the strips and the flour in a plastic bag and toss to coat, shaking off any excess. Heat half the oil in a large frying pan and cook the onion and garlic for 2 minutes, or until golden. Add the mushrooms and cook for a further 3 minutes, then remove from the pan.

2   Heat the remaining oil in the same frying pan, add the beef in batches and cook over medium–high heat for 3–4 minutes, or until browned. Return the onion and mushroom mixture and all the beef to the pan with any juices.

3   Stir in the stock and tomato paste, bring to the boil, then reduce the heat and simmer for 2–3 minutes. Add the sour cream and half the chopped parsley and season to taste with freshly ground black pepper. Mix together well, then serve immediately with steamed rice. Garnish with the remaining parsley.

Green peas are a good source of vegetable protein and fibre. Their sweet flavour and bright colour also makes them a hit with small children.

Pea & ham risotto

1 tablespoon olive oil

1 celery stalk, chopped

2 tablespoons chopped flat-leaf (Italian) parsley

70 g (2½ oz) sliced ham, coarsely chopped

250 g (9 oz/1⅔ cups) peas (fresh or frozen)

125 ml (4 fl oz/½ cup) dry white wine

750 ml (26 fl oz/3 cups) salt-reduced chicken stock

60 g (2¼ oz) unsalted butter

1 brown onion, chopped

440 g (15½ oz/2 cups) arborio rice

35 g (1¼ oz/⅓ cup) grated parmesan cheese, plus extra shavings, to garnish

Prep time 25 minutes

Cooking time 45 minutes

Serves 4

1 Heat the oil in a frying pan, add the celery and parsley and season with freshly ground black pepper. Cook over medium heat for a few minutes to soften the celery. Add the ham and stir for 1 minute. Add the peas and half the wine, bring to the boil, then reduce the heat and simmer, uncovered, until almost all the liquid has evaporated. Set aside.

2 Put the stock and 750 ml (26 fl oz/3 cups) water in a separate saucepan and keep at simmering point.

3 Heat the butter in a large heavy-based saucepan. Add the onion and stir until softened. Add the rice and stir well. Pour in the remaining wine; allow it to bubble and evaporate. Add 125 ml (4 fl oz/½ cup) hot stock to the rice mixture. Stir constantly over low heat, with a wooden spoon, until all the stock has been absorbed. Repeat the process until all the stock has been added and the rice is creamy and tender (it may take about 20–25 minutes).

4 Add the pea mixture and parmesan and serve immediately. Serve with the extra parmesan shavings and some freshly ground black pepper.

hint If fresh peas are in season, 500 g (1 lb 2 oz) peas in the pod will yield about 250 g (9 oz/1⅔ cups) shelled peas.

Rice is a great food for kids to demonstrate their developing cutlery technique.
It's still a messy business at this stage, so be patient!

Baked chicken & leek risotto

2 tablespoons olive oil

1 leek, thinly sliced

2 boneless, skinless chicken breasts, finely chopped

440 g (15½ oz/2 cups) arborio rice

60 ml (2 fl oz/¼ cup) white wine

1.25 litres (44 fl oz/5 cups) salt-reduced chicken stock

35 g (1¼ oz/⅓ cup) grated parmesan cheese, plus extra, to garnish

2 tablespoons thyme, plus extra, to garnish

Prep time 10 minutes

Cooking time 40 minutes

Serves 4–6

1 Preheat the oven to 150°C (300°F/Gas 2). Heat the oil in a 5 litre (175 fl oz/20 cups) ovenproof dish with a lid over medium heat, add the leek and cook for 2 minutes, or until softened but not browned.

2 Add the chicken and cook, stirring, for 2–3 minutes, or until it is golden on both sides. Add the rice and stir so that it is well coated with butter. Cook for 1 minute.

3 Add the wine and stock and bring to the boil. Cover and place in the oven and cook for 30 minutes, stirring halfway through. Remove from the oven and stir through the parmesan and thyme leaves. Season with freshly ground black pepper. Sprinkle with the extra thyme and parmesan and serve.

This curry is a great introduction to the tastes of India for your toddler. Just be certain that the curry paste you buy is a mild one.

Lamb kofta curry

500 g (1 lb 2 oz) lean minced (ground) lamb

1 brown onion, finely chopped

1 garlic clove, crushed

1 teaspoon grated fresh ginger

1 teaspoon garam masala

1 teaspoon ground coriander

40 g (1½ oz/⅓ cup) ground almonds

steamed rice, to serve

Sauce

2 teaspoons oil

1 brown onion, finely chopped

3 tablespoons mild Korma curry paste

400 g (14 oz) tin chopped tomatoes

125 g (4½ oz/½ cup) plain yoghurt

1 teaspoon lemon juice

1 Combine the lamb, onion, garlic, ginger, garam masala, ground coriander and ground almonds in a bowl. Shape the mixture into walnut-sized balls with your hands.

2 Heat a large non-stick frying pan and cook the koftas in batches until brown on both sides—they don't have to be cooked all the way through at this stage.

3 Meanwhile, to make the sauce, heat the oil in a saucepan over low heat. Add the onion and cook for 6–8 minutes, or until soft and golden. Add the curry paste and cook for 1 minute, or until fragrant. Add the chopped tomato and simmer for 5 minutes. Stir in the yoghurt (1 tablespoon at a time) and the lemon juice until combined.

4 Place the koftas in the tomato sauce. Cook, covered, over low heat for 20 minutes. Serve over steamed rice.

Prep time 25 minutes

Cooking time 35 minutes

Serves 4

Letting children get involved in preparing and selecting their food can increase their desire to eat it. So, for a fun meal, let everyone wrap their own rolls.

Fresh spring rolls

½ barbecued (grilled) chicken
   (see hints)

50 g (1¾ oz) dried mung bean
   vermicelli

8 x 17 cm (6½ inch) square dried rice
   paper wrappers

16 Thai basil leaves

1 large handful coriander (cilantro)
   leaves

1 carrot, cut into short thin strips
   and blanched

2 tablespoons plum sauce

Prep time 30 minutes
Cooking time Nil
Makes 8

1 Remove the meat from the chicken carcass, discard the skin and finely shred. Soak the vermicelli in the hot water for 10 minutes and then drain. Dip a rice paper wrapper into warm water until it softens then place it on a clean work surface. Put one-eighth of the chicken in the centre of the wrapper and top with 2 basil leaves, a few coriander leaves, a few carrot strips and a small amount of vermicelli. Spoon a little plum sauce over the top.

2 Press the filling down to flatten it a little, then fold in the two sides and roll it up tightly like a parcel. Lay the roll seam side down, on a serving plate and sprinkle with a little water. Cover with a damp tea towel (dish towel) and repeat the process with the remaining ingredients. Serve with your favourite dipping sauce or a little extra plum sauce.

hints When buying the barbecued (grilled) chicken, ask for two breast quarters. Rice paper wrappers must be kept moist or they become brittle. If you leave the spring rolls for any length of time and they start to dry out, sprinkle cold water on them.

This recipe is great competition for its fast food counterparts because it uses premium ingredients that are nutritious, tasty and fun to eat.

Baked chicken nuggets

40 g (1½ oz/1⅓ cups) corn-based cereal flakes

400 g (14 oz) boneless, skinless chicken breasts

plain (all-purpose) flour, for dusting

1 egg white

Prep time 15 minutes

Cooking time 10 minutes

Serves 4

1 Preheat the oven to 200°C (400°F/Gas 6). Process the corn-based cereal flakes in a food processor, blender or in a mortar with a pestle, to make fine crumbs.

2 Cut the chicken breasts into bite-sized pieces. Toss in seasoned flour then in lightly beaten egg white. Roll each piece in the cereal-flake crumbs until well coated.

3 Lightly grease a baking tray with oil and place the nuggets on it. Bake for 10 minutes, or until golden and cooked through.

baked potato wedges Preheat the oven to 200°C (400°F/Gas 6). Peel and slice 1.3 kg (3 lb) orange sweet potato into 6 x 2 cm (2½ x ¾ inch) wedges. Put the sweet potato wedges in a large roasting tin and toss with 2 tablespoons of olive oil. Bake for about 30 minutes, or until browned and crisp. Serve warm. Serves 4.

Research tells us that the foundations of a child's food preferences are established in the early days of eating. Don't be afraid to allow them to try new and tasty flavours; the experience will pay off when they are older.

Toddler's chilli con carne

2 teaspoons olive oil

1 large brown onion, chopped

1 garlic clove, crushed

2 teaspoons sweet paprika

1 teaspoon dried oregano

2 teaspoons ground cumin

750 g (1 lb 10 oz) lean minced (ground) beef

375 ml (13 fl oz/1½ cups) salt-reduced beef stock

400 g (14 oz) tin diced tomatoes

125 g (4½ oz/½ cup) tomato paste (concentrated purée)

400 g (14 oz) tin kidney beans, drained and rinsed

1 Heat the olive oil in a large saucepan over low heat. Add the onion and cook for 4–5 minutes, or until soft. Stir in the garlic, paprika, oregano and cumin. Increase the heat to medium, add the beef and cook for 5–8 minutes, or until just browned, breaking up any lumps with a spoon.

2 Reduce the heat to low, add the stock, tomato and tomato paste to the pan and cook for 35–45 minutes, stirring frequently.

3 Stir in the kidney beans and simmer for 10 minutes. Serve on its own or over rice.

Prep time 15 minutes
Cooking time 1 hour 10 minutes
Serves 6

Be it laziness or just tired little jaws, toddlers often don't manage meat well. Meat needs to be presented in a way toddlers can manage (without puréeing). Minced (ground) meat, as in this recipe, is the perfect solution.

Chicken meatball soup

spring onion (scallion)

375 g (13 oz) minced (ground) chicken

875 ml (30 fl oz/3½ cups) reduced-salt chicken stock

2 tbsp frozen peas

2 tbsp finely diced carrot

60 g (2¼ oz/½ cup) dried pasta shapes

Prep time 15 minutes
Cooking time 10 minutes
Serves 4

1 Finely chop half the spring onion and thinly slice the remainder. Combine the chicken and finely chopped spring onion until thoroughly mixed, then form the mixture into small balls, about the size of walnuts.

2 Put the stock in a saucepan and bring to the boil. Add the peas, carrot and pasta shapes. Simmer for 3 minutes, or until the vegetables are tender, then add the reserved sliced spring onion.

3 Drop the chicken meatballs into the simmering soup. Cook for about 5 minutes, turning the meatballs in the stock so they cook evenly, or until the meatballs turn white and float to the surface and the pasta is cooked through. Skim off any scum from the surface of the soup before serving.

hint Instead of making the chicken meatballs, you can substitute the minced chicken with the same amount of boneless, skinless chicken breast. Simply cut the chicken into thin slices, place it between two sheets of baking paper and gently pound with a rolling pin to make almost transparent slices. These will cook in seconds in the hot soup.

Couscous is a great staple for any family's pantry. It is made from durum wheat and is already pre-steamed, so it needs only a few minutes to cook.

Vegetable couscous

30 g (1 oz) unsalted butter

1 brown onion, sliced

1 garlic clove, crushed

1 teaspoon ground cumin

2 carrots, thinly sliced

150 g (5½ oz) pumpkin (winter squash), chopped

400 g (14 oz) tin chickpeas, rinsed and drained

400 g (14 oz) tin chopped tomatoes

1 all-purpose potato, chopped

1 small eggplant (aubergine), chopped

60 ml (2 fl oz/¼ cup) salt-reduced vegetable stock

150 g (5½ oz/1¼ cups) green beans, cut into short lengths

2 zucchini (courgettes), cut into chunks

Couscous

250 ml (9 fl oz/1 cup) salt-reduced vegetable stock

185 g (6½ oz/1 cup) instant couscous

30 g (1 oz) unsalted butter

1 Melt the butter in a saucepan over medium heat. Add the onion, garlic and cumin and cook for 2–3 minutes, or until softened.

2 Add the carrot, pumpkin, chickpeas, tomato, potato, eggplant and vegetable stock. Cook for 10 minutes, stirring occasionally. Mix in the beans and zucchini and cook for a further 5 minutes, or until the vegetables are tender.

3 To make the couscous, pour the stock and 60 ml (2 fl oz/¼ cup) water into a saucepan and bring to the boil. Remove from the heat and stir in the couscous and butter. Cover and stand for 5 minutes. Fluff the grains with a fork to separate. Serve the couscous topped with the vegetables, or fold the vegetables through the couscous.

Prep time 20 minutes

Cooking time 30 minutes

Serves 4

Turn meal preparation into an activity to keep toddlers happily occupied. Let them stir the filling, peel the onion or wash the spinach.

Spinach & ricotta cannelloni

375 g (13 oz) fresh lasagne sheets

70 g (2½ oz/½ cup) grated
   mozzarella cheese

50 g (1¾ oz/½ cup) finely grated
   parmesan cheese

Filling

1 tablespoon olive oil

1 small onion, finely chopped

2 garlic cloves, crushed

3 bunches English spinach

300 g (10½ oz/1¼ cups) fresh ricotta

1 tablespoon oregano

Sauce

1 tablespoon olive oil

1 small brown onion, finely chopped

2 garlic cloves, crushed

400 g (14 oz) tin peeled whole
   tomatoes

125 ml (4 fl oz) tomato-based pasta
   sauce

1 teaspoon dried oregano

2 teaspoons Dijon mustard

1 tablespoon balsamic vinegar

1 teaspoon sugar

Prep time 45 minutes

Cooking time 1 hour

Serves 4

1 Preheat the oven to 180°C (350°F/Gas 4).

2 To make the filling, heat the oil in a pan and add the onion and garlic. Cook for 3–5 minutes, or until the onion softens. Trim and finely shred the spinach, add it to the pan and cook for 5 minutes, or until wilted and the moisture has evaporated. Remove from the heat. Once cooled, combine with the ricotta and oregano in a food processor or blender. Process until smooth and season.

3 To make the sauce, heat the oil in a pan, add the onion and garlic and cook over low heat for 8–10 minutes. Add the rest of the sauce ingredients. Bring to the boil, then reduce the heat and simmer for 10–15 minutes, or until the sauce thickens.

4 Cut the lasagne sheets into twelve 12 cm (4½ inch) squares. Lightly grease a 2 litre (70 fl oz/8 cup) ovenproof dish. Spread one-third of the sauce over the base, then spoon 1½ tablespoons of the spinach mixture onto one side of each square of lasagne, leaving a 5 mm (¼ inch) border. Roll up the pasta to cover the filling and place in the dish seam side down. Repeat with all the sheets, spacing the cannelloni evenly in the dish. Spoon over the remaining sauce and sprinkle with the cheeses. Bake for 30–35 minutes, or until the cheese is bubbling and golden. Allow to stand for 5 minutes before serving.

Barbecued (grilled) chickens are a quick and healthy way to add protein to a meal—especially once you have removed the skin.

Chicken pilaff

1 barbecued (grilled) chicken

50 g (1¾ oz) butter

1 brown onion, finely chopped

2 garlic cloves, crushed

300 g (10½ oz/1½ cups) basmati rice

1 tablespoon currants

2 tablespoons finely chopped dried
   apricots

1 teaspoon ground cinnamon

pinch of ground cardamom

750 ml (26 fl oz/3 cups) salt-reduced
   chicken stock

1 small handful coriander (cilantro)
   leaves, chopped

1 Remove the skin and any fat from the chicken and chop the meat into even, bite-sized pieces.

2 Melt the butter in a large, deep frying pan over medium heat. Add the onion and garlic and cook for 2 minutes. Add the rice, currants, apricots and spices and stir until well coated.

3 Pour in the stock and bring to the boil. Reduce the heat to low and simmer, covered, for 15 minutes. Add a little water if it starts to dry out.

4 Stir through the chicken for 1–2 minutes, or until heated through, then stir through the coriander just before serving.

Prep time 15 minutes

Cooking time 20 minutes

Serves 4

Recipes that can be prepared ahead, like this one, are a blessing when dealing with small children. As every parent knows, timing is everything.

Chicken & mushroom spirals

2 tablespoons olive oil

2 slices rindless bacon, cut into thin
strips

2 garlic cloves, crushed

250 g (9 oz) mushrooms, sliced

125 ml (4 fl oz/½ cup) chicken stock

185 ml (6 fl oz/¾ cup) cream
(whipping)

4 spring onions (scallions), chopped

1 tablespoon plain (all-purpose)
flour

2 large cooked boneless, skinless
chicken breasts, chopped

500 g (1 lb 2 oz) spiral pasta

50 g (1¾ oz/½ cup) grated parmesan
cheese

Prep time 10 minutes

Cooking time 20 minutes

Serves 4

1 Heat the oil in a large, deep frying pan over medium heat. Add the bacon, garlic and mushrooms and cook for 2 minutes.

2 Add the stock and cook until the liquid has reduced by half. Add the cream and spring onions, and bring to the boil. Combine the flour and 60 ml (2 fl oz/¼ cup) water until smooth. Add to the pan and stir over the heat until the mixture boils and thickens. Reduce the heat and simmer for 1 minute. Fold through the chicken and cook for 1 minute to heat through. Season with freshly ground black pepper.

3 Cook the pasta in a large saucepan of boiling water, following the packet directions. Drain. Add the pasta to the sauce and toss to mix. Sprinkle with parmesan cheese. Serve with a green salad.

hints Scrub cutting boards thoroughly in hot soapy water to remove all traces of chicken. Make sure wooden boards have a smooth surface. Rough, cracked surfaces can contain bacteria. This sauce can be made 1 day in advance. Reheat the sauce and cook the pasta until *al dente*, just before serving.

Rich in protein from the eggs, beta-carotene from the carrots and sweet potato, and vitamin C from the cabbage, gado gado is a nutritious adventure for toddlers.

Gado gado

3 eggs

2 orange sweet potatoes, cut into 1 cm (½ inch) thick slices

2 potatoes, halved and cut into 1 cm (½ inch) thick slices

125 g (4½ oz) baby (pattypan) squash, halved

250 g (9 oz) cabbage, cut into large pieces

2 carrots, cut into 1 cm (½ inch) thick strips

1 cucumber

125 g (4½ oz/1⅓ cups) fresh bean sprouts, tails removed

Prep time 20 minutes

Cooking time 20 minutes

Serves 6

1 Put the eggs in a saucepan with cold water to cover. Bring to the boil, reduce to a simmer and cook for 10 minutes; stir the water during the first few minutes to centre the yolk. Drain and cool under cold water.

2 Bring a large saucepan of water to the boil. Blanch each type of vegetable separately in the boiling water; they must be firm and not overcooked. The sweet potato and potato will each need about 8–10 minutes; the squash 1 minute; the carrots 2 minutes; and the cabbage 2 minutes. Remove the vegetables from the water with a slotted spoon and plunge into a bowl of iced water to stop the cooking process and set the colour.

3 Drain the vegetables from the iced water and dry briefly on paper towels. Shell the boiled eggs and cut them into quarters. Slice the cucumber into thin strips. Arrange all the vegetables in decorative groups and garnish with the sliced eggs and bean sprouts. Top with peanut sauce (see below).

peanut sauce Heat 1 tablespoon oil in a saucepan and cook 1 finely chopped small brown onion for 5 minutes over low heat, or until soft and lightly golden. Add 125 g (4½ oz/½ cup) smooth peanut butter, 185 ml (6 fl oz/¾ cup) coconut milk, 1 tablespoon lemon juice, 1 tablespoon salt-reduced dark soy sauce and 60 ml (2 fl oz/¼ cup) water, and stir well. Bring to the boil, stirring constantly, then reduce the heat and simmer for 5 minutes, or until the sauce has reduced and thickened.

If you crumb the veal while your toddler is sleeping, this can become another quick and nutritious meal to serve up with their favourite vegetables.

Veal schnitzel

4 thin veal steaks

100 g (3⅓ oz/1 cup) dry breadcrumbs

½ teaspoon dried basil (optional)

25 g (1 oz/¼ cup) grated parmesan cheese

plain (all-purpose) flour, for coating

1 egg, lightly beaten

1 tablespoon milk

oilve oil, for frying

Prep time 20 minutes + 30 minutes chilling

Cooking time 5 minutes

Serves 4

1 Trim the meat of any excess fat. Place the veal between sheets of plastic wrap and flatten with a meat mallet or rolling pin until 3 mm (⅛ inch) thick. Nick the edges to prevent curling. Combine the breadcrumbs, basil, if using, and parmesan on a sheet of baking paper.

2 Coat the veal steaks in flour, shaking off the excess. Combine the beaten egg and milk. Working with one at a time, dip the steaks into the egg mixture, then coat with the breadcrumb mixture. Lightly shake off the excess. Refrigerate for 30 minutes to firm the coating.

3 Heat the oil in a large frying pan and cook the veal steaks over medium heat for 2–3 minutes on each side, or until golden and cooked through. Drain on paper towels and serve.

Meat on the bone is tender, tasty and particularly popular with toddlers. Finely chop the meat for reluctant chewers, but leave some meat on the bone for them to gnaw on.

Lamb cutlets with mash

2 teaspoons oil

2 French trimmed lamb cutlets

Mash

100 g (3½ oz) small new potatoes, chopped

½ small garlic clove, chopped

40 g (1½ oz/¼ cup) frozen peas

5 g (⅛ oz) margarine

1 tablespoon milk

Prep time 5 minutes

Cooking time 5 minutes

Serves 1

1 To make the mash, bring a small saucepan of water to the boil and cook the potato and garlic for 4 minutes. Add the peas and cook for a further 1 minute or until the potato is soft. Drain, return to the saucepan and mash with the margarine. Stir through the milk and keep warm.

2 Meanwhile, heat the oil in a small frying pan and cook the cutlets over medium heat for 2 minutes. Turn and cook for a further 1 minute, or until done to your liking. Serve with the mash.

hint Some toddlers will use the cutlet bone as a handle and chew the meat away from the bone. For smaller toddlers, remove the meat from the bone, chop into small pieces and stir through the mash.

Take advantage of daytime sleeps to get this recipe on the stove. Come dinnertime, all that needs to be prepared is the accompaniment. Osso buco is rich in protein, vitamins and the minerals iron and zinc.

Osso buco

8 large veal shanks, sliced

plain (all-purpose) flour, for dusting

20 g (¾ oz) unsalted butter

60 ml (2 fl oz/¼ cup) oil

1 brown onion, finely chopped

1 carrot, finely diced

1 celery stalk, finely diced

1 bay leaf

2 garlic cloves, crushed

250 ml (9 fl oz/1 cup) red wine (optional)

1 litre (35 fl oz/4 cups) salt-reduced beef stock

400 g (14 oz) tin diced tomatoes

Prep time 20 minutes

Cooking time 2 hours 50 minutes

Serves 6

1 Lightly dust the veal shanks in flour, shaking off the excess. Heat the butter and 2 tablespoons of the oil in a large heavy-based saucepan or casserole dish over high heat. Add the veal and cook in two batches for 2–3 minutes on each side, or until golden. Remove from the pan.

2 Reduce the heat to low and add the remaining oil to the pan. Heat, then add the onion, carrot, celery and bay leaf and cook over low heat for about 10 minutes, or until softened and golden. Add the garlic and wine, if using, increase the heat and boil for 3–4 minutes.

3 Add the stock and tomato and return the veal to the saucepan. Bring to the boil, then reduce the heat and simmer for 2½ hours, or until the meat is very tender.

4 Serve with mashed potato or steamed rice.

hint This recipe works with other less expensive cuts such as lamb forequarter pieces. If you are not using red wine, add an extra 250 ml (9 fl oz/1 cup) stock.

Snacks & drinks

For healthy pastry snacks, choose pastry made from good oils such as canola, olive, sunflower or safflower oil. It will make these cheese bites much healthier for little people—and big ones too.

Crunchy cheese bites

250 g (9 oz/2 cups) grated cheddar cheese

125 g (4½ oz) feta cheese, crumbled

60 g (2¼ oz/¼ cup) ricotta cheese

30 g (1 oz/¼ cup) chopped spring onions (scallions)

1 small tomato, chopped

1 egg, beaten

4 sheets ready-rolled puff pastry

beaten egg, to brush

milk, to brush

Prep time 15 minutes

Cooking time 15 minutes

Makes about 20

1 Preheat the oven to 220°C (425°F/Gas 7). Combine the cheeses, spring onion, tomato and egg in a bowl. Season with freshly ground black pepper.

2 Cut the pastry into rounds using a 10 cm (4 inch) cutter. Place heaped teaspoons of the mixture onto one half of each round.

3 Fold the pastry over the filling to make semi-circles, brush the edges between the pastry with a little of the beaten egg and press the edges together firmly with a fork to seal.

4 Place on a baking tray and brush with a little milk. Bake in the oven for 10–15 minutes, or until puffed and golden. Allow the pastries to cool for at least 10 minutes before serving.

cheesy pinwheels Alternatively, divide the cheese mixture from the recipe above into two and spread over 2 sheets of puff pastry, leaving a 1 cm (½ inch) border. Roll up firmly and trim the ends. Cut into 1.5 cm (⅝ inch) lengths and place on a lined baking tray. Bake for about 12–15 minutes, or until the pastry is puffed and golden. Cool for 5 minutes before removing from the tray, then serve warm. Makes 24.

Snacks for toddlers don't need to be complicated, but they do need to be made from healthy ingredients. This snack certainly fits the bill.

Vegetables with tzatziki dip

selection of sliced blanched
    vegetables (see hints), to serve

Dip

2 Lebanese (short) cucumbers,
    deseeded and grated

185 g (6½ oz/¾ cup) plain yoghurt

2 garlic cloves, crushed

1 teaspoon lemon juice

1 teaspoon chopped dill

½ teaspoon chopped mint

Prep time 15 minutes

Cooking time Nil

Serves 4

1 To make the dip, wrap the grated cucumber in a tea towel (dish towel) and squeeze out the excess water.

2 Mix the cucumber with the remaining dip ingredients and serve with the sliced vegetables. If you like, offer some poppadoms or chunks of bread.

hints Choose your favourite vegetables or a selection that might include cauliflower, baby corn, broccoli, spring onion (scallion), beans, snow peas (mangetout), mushrooms, celery, zucchini (courgette), cucumber, capsicum (pepper), carrot and cherry tomatoes. Some vegetables, such as celery, cucumber, zucchini (courgette) and carrot, will be extra crisp if refrigerated in a bowl of iced water before use. Other vegetables may soften if left in water.

sour cream dip Combine 250 g (9 oz/1 cup) sour cream with ¼ teaspoon snipped dill, a pinch of sugar and 2 tablespoons thickened (whipping) cream. Pour into a small dish and place in the centre of a serving platter. Surround with a selection of blanched vegetables.

Young toddlers will probably prefer to dip their fingers into the hummus. But as they get older, they will enjoy dipping with pieces of pitta bread or vegetable sticks. Vegetable chips are also a great accompaniment to hummus.

Pitta bread with hummus

220 g (7¾ oz/1 cup) dried chickpeas

80 ml (2½ fl oz/⅓ cup) olive oil

3–4 tablespoons lemon juice

2 garlic cloves, crushed

2 tablespoons tahini

1 tablespoon ground cumin

pitta bread, to serve

Prep time 15 minutes + 8 hours
  soaking

Cooking time 1 hour

Serves 4

1 Soak the chickpeas in water for 8 hours or overnight. Drain. Put in a saucepan, cover with cold water, bring to the boil and cook for around 50–60 minutes. Drain, reserving 185–250 ml (6–9 fl oz/¾–1 cup) of the cooking liquid.

2 Place the chickpeas in a food processor with the oil, lemon juice, garlic, tahini and cumin. Blend well until the mixture begins to look thick and creamy. With the motor running, gradually add the reserved cooking liquid until the mixture reaches the desired consistency. Serve with pitta bread, raw or blanched vegetables or vegetable chips (see below). You can also use it as a spread for sandwiches.

vegetable chips Preheat the oven to 180°C (350°F/Gas 4). Peel the skin of 500 g (1 lb 2 oz) each orange sweet potato, beetroot (beet) and parsnip. Run a vegetable peeler along the length of the sweet potato and beetroot to make thin ribbons. Cut the parsnip into thin slices. Fill a deep heavy-based saucepan one-third full of oil and heat to 190°C (375°F), or until a cube of bread dropped into the oil browns in 10 seconds. Cook the vegetables in batches for about 30 seconds, or until golden and crisp, turning with tongs if necessary. Drain on crumpled paper towels. Keep warm on a baking tray in the oven and cook the remaining chips (fries). Serve with the hummus.

These delicious muffins couldn't be easier to make, and they offer a great opportunity for eager toddlers to lend a hand in the kitchen.

Easy berry muffins

250 g (9 oz/1 cup) plain yoghurt

100 g (3½ oz/1 cup) rolled (porridge) oats

60 ml (2 fl oz/¼ cup) oil

80 g (2¾ oz/⅓ cup) caster (superfine) sugar

1 egg

125 g (4½ oz/1 cup) self-raising flour, sifted

3 teaspoons baking powder

300 g (10½ oz/1⅓ cups) mixed frozen berries, thawed

1 Preheat the oven to 180°C (350°F/Gas 4). Place paper cases into 16 muffin holes. Mix together the yoghurt, oats, oil, caster sugar and egg. Gently stir in the sifted flour and baking powder with the fruit.

2 Spoon the mixture into paper cases in the muffin tin and bake for 20–25 minutes or until golden brown and a skewer comes out clean when inserted into the centre.

hint Muffins can be made with any number of delicious fruit-based combinations. Aside from berry combinations, apple, sultanas (golden raisins) and cinnamon, or pear and date can make a tasty alternative.

Prep time 10 minutes

Cooking time 25 minutes

Makes 16 muffins

Because of their small tummies and high nutrition needs, every meal in a toddler's diet needs to count—including snacks. These biscuits hit the spot, combining the goodness of rolled oats and dried fruits.

Muesli crunch biscuits

125 g (4½ oz) unsalted butter

90 g (3¼ oz/½ cup) soft brown sugar

a few drops natural vanilla extract

1 egg

75 g (23/4 oz/½ cup) wholemeal (whole-wheat) self-raising flour

400 g (14 oz/3 cups) untoasted muesli (granola), without nuts

125 g (4½ oz/⅔ cup) chopped dried apricots

Prep time 20 minutes

Cooking time 15 minutes

Makes 24

1 Preheat the oven to 190°C (375°F/Gas 5). Lightly grease two large baking trays.

2 Cream the butter and sugar together, then add the vanilla and egg and beat well. Sift in the flour, add the muesli and stir in the chopped apricots. Shape the biscuit (cookie) mixture into balls, then place on the prepared trays and flatten lightly with a fork. Bake for about 10–12 minutes, or until lightly golden. Cool on a wire cooling rack, then store in an airtight container.

variation Use corn-based cereal flakes or bran flakes instead of some of the muesli, and mix the chopped apricots with other dried fruits.

Muffins are a good way to get extra fruit or vegies into your toddler's diet. Sweet corn is a good source of beta-carotene and B vitamins, especially niacin.

Corn & ham muffins

oil, for brushing

125 g (4½ oz/1 cup) self-raising flour

40 g (1½ oz/¼ cup) chopped ham

60 g (2¼ oz/⅓ cup) tin corn kernels, drained

¼ red capsicum (pepper), deseeded and finely chopped

2 teapoons chopped parsley

60 g (2¼ oz) margarine, melted

125 ml (4 fl oz/½ cup) milk

1 egg

1 tablespoon sesame seeds

Prep time 10 minutes
Cooking time 20 minutes
Makes 24

1 Preheat the oven to 210°C (415°C/Gas 6–7). Brush two 12-hole mini muffin tins with oil. Sift the flour into a large bowl. Add the ham, corn, capsicum and parsley and stir to combine.

2 In a small bowl, combine the melted margarine, milk and egg. Make a well in the centre of the flour mixture and add the milk mixture. Mix the dough lightly with a fork or rubber spatula until the ingredients are just combined. (Do not overmix; the batter should be quite lumpy.)

3 Spoon the mixture into the prepared tins. Sprinkle the muffins with the sesame seeds. Bake the muffins for 15–20 minutes, or until golden. Cool on a wire rack.

variations If you prefer, replace white flour with wholemeal (whole-wheat) flour. A little extra milk may be required as wholemeal flour absorbs more liquid. Try adding other vegetables instead of the corn and capsicum, such as half a grated carrot and zucchini (courgette). For a vegetarian option, replace the ham with chopped, semi-dried (sun-blushed) tomatoes.

A nutritious drink like this is often all a toddler needs as a snack, especially when it's made with bananas, which have twice the vitamin C of apples and pears.

Banana smoothie

1 banana

1 tablespoon plain yoghurt

1 teaspoon honey (optional,
    only for children over 12 months)

250 ml (9 fl oz/1 cup) milk

Prep time 5 minutes

Cooking time Nil

Serves 2

1 Peel the banana and roughly chop. Place in a blender with the yoghurt, honey, if using, and milk and blend until smooth, thick and creamy.

2 Pour into two glasses and serve.

hint The secret to the success of this smoothie is the preparation of the banana. The smoothie will be thicker and, as a result, more delicious if the banana is peeled and frozen for at least half an hour before it is used.

variation Mangoes also work well in this smoothie, either as an accompaniment or added to the smoothie with the banana. Alternatively, you can add tin peaches or apricots along with the banana for a delightful tangy taste.

A universal favourite, these carbohydrate-rich pikelets (griddle cakes) are bite-sized energy food for small children on the go.

Junior pikelets

125 g (4½ oz/1 cup) self-raising flour

¼ teaspoon bicarbonate of soda (baking soda)

2 tablespoons caster (superfine) sugar

125 ml (4 fl oz/½ cup) milk

1 egg

2 teaspoons oil, plus extra for greasing

60 g (2¼ oz/½ cup) sultanas (golden raisins)

Prep time 10 minutes

Cooking time 15 minutes

Makes 24

1 Sift the flour and bicarbonate of soda together into a bowl. Stir in the sugar. In a small bowl, combine the milk, egg and oil. Make a well in the centre and whisk in the milk mixture to make a smooth batter. Add the sultanas to the mixture and mix well.

2 Lightly grease and heat a frying pan with oil. Drop teaspoons of the batter into the pan and cook until bubbles form. Turn and cook the other side of the pikelet (griddle cake) until golden. Cool on a wire rack, then serve warm with butter or margarine. These pikelets be frozen, layered between sheets of baking paper, for up to 1 month.

For the reluctant milk drinker, there is nothing wrong with adding flavouring to encourage enjoyment. Research has shown that children who drink milk are often taller and have healthier bones and body weights than those who don't.

Vanilla milkshake

500 ml (17 fl oz/2 cups) milk,
   well chilled

1 teaspoon natural vanilla extract

sugar, to taste

Prep time 5 minutes
Cooking time Nil
Serves 2

1 Put the milk, vanilla extract and sugar into a large bowl or blender and whisk or blend for 20 seconds to combine.

2 Pour into two long cups and serve with straws for fun.

hint Milkshakes can be made using an electric blender, a whisk or a hand-held beater, or the ingredients can be placed in a tall sealed container and shaken until frothy.

variation Your toddler's favourite fruit can be added to this recipe, but it will need to be processed first in a blender to make it smooth.

This recipe is a much healthier alternative to fruit juice as it has around four times the fibre of most commercial juices.

Fresh fruit slushy

90 g (3¼ oz) fresh pineapple, peeled and cored

1 banana

3 kiwi fruit, sliced

250 ml (9 fl oz/1 cup) unsweetened tropical fruit juice

2 ice cubes

1 Cut the pineapple and banana into chunks. Put in a blender with the kiwi fruit, fruit juice and ice cubes and blend until smooth.

2 Pour into four cups and serve.

Prep time 10 minutes

Cooking time Nil

Serves 4

Desserts & party food

Sago is made from the dried starchy granules found in the pith of Indonesian palm trees. Its unique texture will likely spark the interest of young eaters.

Apple sago pudding

80 g (2¾ oz/⅓ cup) caster (superfine) sugar

100 g (3½ oz/½ cup) sago

600 ml (21 fl oz) milk

40 g (1½ oz/⅓ cup) sultanas (golden raisins)

1 teaspoon natural vanilla extract

a pinch of ground nutmeg

¼ teaspoon ground cinnamon

2 eggs, lightly beaten

3 small apples (about 250 g/9 oz), peeled, cored and very thinly sliced

1 tablespoon soft brown sugar

Prep time 15 minutes

Cooking time 50 minutes

Serves 4

1 Preheat the oven to 180°C (350°F/Gas 4). Grease a 1.5 litre (52 fl oz/6 cup) ceramic soufflé dish. Place the sugar, sago, milk and sultanas in a saucepan. Heat the mixture, stirring often. Bring to the boil, then reduce the heat and simmer for 5 minutes.

2 Stir in the vanilla extract, nutmeg, cinnamon, egg and apple slices, then pour into the prepared dish. Sprinkle with the brown sugar and bake for 45 minutes, or until set and golden brown.

This is a wholesome sweet treat based upon bread, milk, eggs and fruit. It can be made even more nutritious if you use fibre-rich bread.

Bread & butter pudding

margarine or butter, for greasing

6 slices wholemeal (whole-wheat) bread

750 ml (26 fl oz/3 cups) milk

¼ teaspoon grated lemon zest

110 g (3¾ oz/½ cup) sugar

4 eggs

125 g (4½ oz/¾ cup) mixed dried fruits such as sultanas (golden raisins), raisins, chopped dried apricots, currants and mixed peel (mixed candied citrus peel)

1 Preheat the oven to 180°C (350°F/Gas 4). Grease an ovenproof dish. Remove the crusts from the bread and thickly spread with margarine or butter.

2 Heat the milk in a saucepan and add the lemon zest. Bring to the boil, then cover and remove from the heat, leaving to infuse for 10 minutes. Beat the sugar and eggs together, then strain the milk over the eggs and mix well.

3 Scatter half the dried fruit over the bottom of the prepared dish and arrange the bread, buttered sides down, on top. Pour in half the custard, then repeat with the remaining fruit, bread and custard. Place the dish in a baking tin and add enough water to fill halfway up the outside of the dish. Bake for 35 minutes.

Prep time 20 minutes +
  10 minutes standing
Cooking time 35 minutes
Serves 4

Besides being a good source of vitamin C and energy-giving carbohydrates, bananas are a great, easy-to-handle fruit for kids.

Choc-banana bites

5 wooden iceblock (popsicle/ice lolly) sticks, cut in half

3 large bananas, peeled and cut into 3 pieces

125 g (4½ oz) dark cooking chocolate, chopped

Prep time 10 minutes + 4 hours freezing

Cooking time 5 minutes

Makes 9

1 Line a 33 x 28 cm (13 x 11¼ inch) baking tray with foil. Carefully push a half-stick into each piece of banana. Place on the prepared tray and freeze for 2 hours or until firm.

2 Put the chocolate in a small heatproof bowl. Stand the bowl over a saucepan of simmering water and stir until the chocolate has melted and is smooth.

3 Working with one banana piece at a time, dip each piece into the hot chocolate mixture, turning to fully coat. Drain off any excess chocolate. Place the banana pieces on the prepared tray. Refrigerate until the chocolate has set, then wrap in plastic wrap and place in the freezer for at least 2 hours to harden. Serve frozen.

New and unusual ways to eat fruit will always appeal to a curious toddler, so these fruit kebabs should be a hit!

Frozen fruit kebabs

140 g (5 oz) fresh pineapple

½ mango

80 g (2¾ oz) seedless watermelon

100 g (3½ oz) rockmelon or any orange-fleshed melon

4 iceblock (popsicle/ice lolly) sticks

1 Remove the skin from all the fruit and cut each type into four cubes. Thread onto the iceblock sticks and freeze for 4 hours or until frozen. To serve, remove from the freezer 10 minutes before eating to allow them to soften slightly.

hint Extra quantities of this recipe can be made and kept in the freezer for a hot day.

Prep time 10 minutes +
  4 hours freezing
Cooking time Nil
Makes 4

This sweet snack is a good source of calcium and fibre. Try freezing some into iceblock (popsicle/ice lolly) moulds for healthy treats on hot days.

Frozen fruit yoghurt

60 g (2¼ oz/½ cup) fresh fruit salad such as pineapple, apple, banana, peach, apricot and/or orange

125 g (4½ oz/½ cup) plain yoghurt

1 Put the fruit salad in a blender, add the yoghurt and purée. Pour the mixture into a freezer tray and freeze.

2 For a lighter texture, remove the mixture from the freezer, return to the blender and whip, then refreeze. Repeat once more.

Prep time 5 minutes +
  4 hours freezing
Cooking time Nil
Serves 2

These yummy little tarts are rich with the goodness of cheese and egg, and if you choose a shortcrust (pie) pastry made with healthy fats (canola or sunflower oils), then birthday treats are as healthy as they can be.

Cheese & bacon tarts

oil spray, for greasing

2 sheets ready-rolled shortcrust (pie) pastry

2 slices bacon, finely chopped

1 small brown onion, finely chopped

125 ml (4 fl oz/½ cup) cream (whipping)

1 egg

½ teaspoon mild mustard

60 g (2¼ oz/½ cup) grated cheddar cheese

Prep time 30 minutes

Cooking time 15 minutes

Makes 18

1 Preheat the oven to 180°C (350°F/Gas 4). Spray two 12-hole mini muffin tins with the oil.

2 Lay out the pastry on a lightly floured work surface. Cut out rounds with a 7 cm (2¾ inch) fluted cutter. Ease the pastry rounds into the muffin holes. Sprinkle the chopped bacon and onion over the pastry shells. Combine the cream, egg and mustard in a small bowl and whisk until smooth. Spoon 1 teaspoon of the mixture into each pastry case. Sprinkle with the grated cheese. Bake the tarts for 15 minutes, or until golden and crisp. Serve warm.

variation If you like, you can substitute drained and flaked tin salmon for the chopped bacon.

Prepared ahead and frozen, home-made sausage rolls are as convenient as ready-made ones. They will be lower in saturated fat if you choose a puff pastry made with healthier fats.

Sausage rolls

1 teaspoon oil, plus extra,
   for greasing

1 brown onion, finely chopped

500 g (1 lb 2 oz) sausage mince
   (meat)

80 g (2¾ oz/1 cup) soft white
   breadcrumbs

2 tablespoons tomato sauce
   (ketchup)

1 egg, lightly beaten

2 sheets frozen ready-rolled puff
   pastry, thawed

beaten egg or milk, for glazing

Prep time 35 minutes

Cooking time 30 minutes

Makes 48

1   Preheat the oven to 210°C (415°F/Gas 6–7). Lightly grease a baking tray with oil.

2   Heat the oil in a frying pan. Add the onion and cook, over low heat, for 2–3 minutes, or until soft and transparent. Put the onion, meat, breadcrumbs, tomato sauce and egg into a bowl and mix together.

3   Lay the pastry sheets on a lightly floured work surface and cut into three horizontal strips. Divide the meat mixture into six equal portions and place across the long edge of the pastry. Roll the pastry up to form long sausage shapes. Brush lightly with a little beaten egg or milk. Cut the rolls into 4 cm (1½ inch) lengths and place on the prepared tray.

4   Bake for 10 minutes, then reduce the heat to 180°C (350°F/Gas 4) and bake for a further 15 minutes, or until golden.

hint   These sausage rolls can be frozen for up to 2 weeks before serving. Thaw and reheat them in a 180°C (350°F/Gas 4) oven for around 15–20 minutes, or until hot.

These mini burgers will best suit older toddlers who are able to hold and eat them, rather than younger children. However, that doesn't mean that they won't enjoy dissecting them and eating each piece separately!

Baby burgers

500 g (1 lb 2 oz) minced (ground) beef

1 small brown onion, finely chopped

1 tablespoon finely chopped flat-leaf (Italian) parsley

1 egg, lightly beaten

1 tablespoon tomato sauce (ketchup)

2 tablespoons oil

1/2 lettuce, finely shredded

2 small tomatoes, thinly sliced

10 small bread rolls, halved

5 cheese slices, halved

5 tin pineapple rings, drained and halved

tomato sauce (ketchup) or barbecue sauce

1 Combine the beef, onion, parsley, beaten egg and tomato sauce in a large bowl. Using your hands, mix until well combined. Divide the mixture into 10 portions. Shape into round patties.

2 Heat the oil in a large, heavy-based pan over medium heat. Cook the patties for 5 minutes on each side, or until they are well browned and cooked through. Remove and drain on paper towels.

3 To assemble the burger, put the lettuce and tomato on the base of the roll. Top with the meat patty, cheese slice and pineapple slice. Add the tomato or barbecue sauce and cover with the remaining roll half. Serve immediately.

Prep time 30 minutes
Cooking time 10 minutes
Makes 10

These tasty pastries look just like sausage rolls, except that they are packed with the goodness of vegetables and cheese. Serve them with tomato sauce (ketchup).

Vegie puffs

Prep time 15 minutes
Cooking time 15 minutes
Makes 12

1 small all-purpose potato, diced
1 small carrot, diced
1 zucchini (courgette), diced
1 celery stalk, diced
40 g (1½ oz/¼ cup) diced pumpkin (winter squash)
15 g (½ oz/¼ cup) chopped broccoli
15 g (½ oz/¼ cup) chopped cauliflower
250 g (9 oz/2 cups) grated cheddar cheese
1 sheet frozen, ready-rolled puff pastry, halved
milk, to brush pastry

1 Put the vegetables in a small saucepan and add enough water to cover. Bring to the boil, then reduce the heat and simmer for 3 minutes. Drain well and transfer the vegetables to a bowl to cool. Add the cheese and mix well.

2 Preheat the oven to 220°C (425°F/Gas 7). Lay the two pieces of pastry on a work surface, divide the mixture in half and spread it along the long side of each piece.

3 Roll up the pastry to form a sausage shape, brush the edge with a little milk and press to seal.

4 Cut each roll into six even-sized pieces. Make a small slit in the centre of each and place on a lightly greased baking tray. Brush with milk and bake for 10 minutes, or until crisp and golden.

These little parcels are a fun, easy-to-hold food with a great crunch factor. This recipe also gives you the option of making them more exotic by using Asian flavourings (don't forget that this will add more salt).

Money bags

1 tablespoon peanut oil

4 spring onions (scallions), finely chopped

2 garlic cloves, crushed

1 tablespoon grated fresh ginger

150 g (5½ oz) minced (ground) chicken

150 g (5½ oz) minced (ground) pork

2 teaspoons salt-reduced soy sauce

2 teaspoons soft brown sugar

2 teaspoons lime juice (optional)

2 teaspoons fish sauce (optional)

3 tablespoons finely chopped coriander (cilantro) leaves

30 won ton wrappers

oil, for deep-frying

garlic chives, for tying

Prep time 30 minutes + cooling time

Cooking time 15 minutes

Makes 30

1 Heat a wok over medium heat, add the oil and swirl to coat. Add the spring onions, garlic and ginger and cook for 1–2 minutes, or until the onions are soft. Add the meats and cook for 4 minutes, or until cooked, breaking up the lumps.

2 Stir in the soy sauce, brown sugar, lime juice and fish sauce, if using, and coriander. Cook, stirring, for 1–2 minutes, or until mixed and dry. Set aside to cool.

3 Place 2 teaspoons of filling in the centre of each won ton wrapper, then lightly brush the edges with water. Lift the sides up tightly and pinch around the filling to form a bag. Trim the edges if necessary.

4 Fill a clean wok one-third full of oil and heat to 190°C (375°F), or until a cube of bread dropped in the oil browns in 10 seconds. Cook the money bags in batches for 30–60 seconds, or until golden and crisp. Drain on crumpled paper towels, then tie with the chives to serve.

Cakes can always be made healthier for kids by using a fruit base and wholemeal (whole-wheat) flour, as we have done in this recipe.

Apple & orange mini cakes

90 g (3¼ oz) unsalted butter

125 g (4½ oz/⅔ cup) soft brown sugar

1 tablespoon honey

1 egg

270 g (9½ oz/1 cup) apple sauce or puréed tin pie apples

125 g (4½ oz/1 cup) wholemeal (whole-wheat) self-raising flour

60 g (2¼ oz/½ cup) self-raising flour

1 teaspoon ground cinnamon

a pinch of ground cloves

Prep time 20 minutes
Cooking time 20 minutes
Makes 36

1 Preheat the oven to 180°C (350°F/Gas 4).

2 Place 36 paper cases on a baking tray. Beat the butter, sugar and honey together until light and creamy, then add the egg and apple sauce and beat until well combined. Sift in the flours and spices and mix well. Spoon the mixture into the paper cases and bake for about 20 minutes, or until a skewer comes out clean when inserted into the centre. Allow to cool and cover with orange glaze icing (see below).

orange glaze icing To make the icing (frosting), combine 125 g (4½ oz/1 cup) icing (confectioners') sugar, 10 g (¼ oz) butter, 1 teaspoon orange zest and 2 tablespoons orange juice in a heatproof bowl to make a soft pouring consistency. Add a little more orange juice if needed. Stand over a saucepan of simmering water and stir until smooth and glossy. Remove from the heat. Allow to cool slightly, then ice the cakes.

Bite-sized and easy-to-eat foods, like these meatballs, make great party food, especially when toddlers have so many better things to do than eat!

Meatballs

375 g (13 oz) minced (ground) beef

1 small brown onion, finely chopped

40 g (1½ oz/½ cup) fresh
    breadcrumbs

1 tablespoon tomato paste
    (concentrated purée)

1 teaspoon worcestershire sauce

1 egg, lightly beaten

2 tablespoons oil

1 Put the beef, onion, breadcrumbs, tomato paste, sauce and egg in a large bowl. Using your hands, mix until well combined. Shape level tablespoons of mixture into balls.

2 Heat the oil in a large frying pan. Add the meatballs and cook over medium heat, shaking the pan often, for 10 minutes, or until the meatballs are cooked and evenly browned. Drain on paper towels. Serve hot or cold with tomato sauce (ketchup), if desired.

Prep time 15 minutes

Cooking time 10 minutes

Makes 25

These crisp, crunchy, butter-flavoured biscuits are popular with small children, especially when they come in fancy shapes.

Shortbreads

250 g (9 oz/2 cups) plain (all-purpose) flour

2 tablespoons rice flour

115 g (4 oz/½ cup) caster (superfine) sugar

250 g (9 oz) unsalted butter, chopped

Prep time 15 minutes

Cooking time 30 minutes

Makes 16

1 Preheat the oven to 160°C (315°F/Gas 2–3). Lightly grease 2 baking trays. Sift the flours together into a large bowl and mix in the sugar. Rub in the butter using your fingertips and press the mixture together.

2 Turn out onto a lightly floured work surface and knead gently. Press out into a round about 1 cm (½ inch) thick and cut out with shaped cutters. Put the shortbreads onto the prepared baking trays. Bake for 25–30 minutes, or until golden brown.

3 Leave to cool on the trays for 5 minutes and then transfer to a wire rack to cool completely. Store in an airtight container.

Not many toddlers can resist helping out when it comes to baking. Let them put the paper cases into the muffin tin, help pour measured ingredients into the mixing bowl and, of course, lick the beaters when it is all done!

Butterfly cupcakes

25 g (4½ oz) unsalted butter, softened

170 g (6 oz/¾ cup) caster (superfine) sugar

185 g (6½ oz/1½ cups) self-raising flour

125 ml (4 fl oz/½ cup) milk

2 eggs

125 ml (4 fl oz/½ cup) thickened (whipping) cream

1½ tablespoons strawberry jam

icing (confectioners') sugar, to dust

Prep time 10 minutes
Cooking time 20 minutes
Makes 18

1   Preheat the oven to 180°C (350°F/Gas 4). Line 18 holes in two muffin tins with paper cases. Beat the butter, sugar, flour, milk and eggs with electric beaters on low speed. Increase the speed and beat until smooth and pale. Divide the mixture evenly among the cases and bake for 30 minutes, or until cooked and golden. Transfer to a wire rack to cool.

2   Cut shallow rounds from the centre of each cake using the point of a sharp knife, then cut the rounds in half. Spoon 2 teaspoons cream into each cavity, top with 1 teaspoon jam and position two halves of the cake tops in the jam to resemble butterfly wings. Dust with icing sugar.

3   Alternatively, do not cut out the centre of the cake and cover each cupcake with buttercream or chocolate buttercream (see below).

buttercream With electric beaters, beat 125 g (4½ oz) unsalted butter until pale and fluffy. Continue beating and gradually add 1 teaspoon natural vanilla extract and 185 g (6½ oz/1½ cups) sifted icing (confectioners') sugar. Gradually add 2 tablespoons milk, at room temperature. Beat the mixture until smooth.

chocolate buttercream To make chocolate buttercream, mix 2 tablespoons sifted unsweetened cocoa powder into the mixture above.

If you can handle the 'help' when making your gingerbread characters, offer a small amount of dough to your toddler and let them roll and cut their own shapes.

Gingerbread people

125 g (4½ oz) unsalted butter

90 g (3¼ oz/½ cup) soft brown sugar

115 g (4 oz/⅓ cup) golden syrup (dark corn syrup)

1 egg

250 g (9 oz/2 cups) plain (all-purpose) flour

40 g (1½ oz/⅓ cup) self-raising flour

1 tablespoon ground ginger

1 teaspoon bicarbonate of soda (baking soda)

Icing

1 egg white

½ teaspoon lemon juice

125 g (4½ oz/1 cup) icing (confectioners') sugar

food colourings

Prep time 30 minutes + 15 minutes refrigeration

Cooking time 15 minutes

Makes 15–20, depending on size of cutters

1 Line two or three baking trays with baking paper. Using electric beaters, beat the butter, sugar and syrup in a large bowl until light and creamy. Add the egg and beat well.

2 Sift in the flours, ginger and bicarbonate of soda. Use a knife to mix until just combined.

3 Use a well-floured hand to gather the dough into a ball. Knead gently on a well-floured surface until smooth. Don't over-handle the dough or it will become tough.

4 Lay a sheet of baking paper over a large chopping board. Roll out the dough on the lined board to a 5 mm (¼ inch) thickness. Preheat the oven to 180°C (350°F/Gas 4).

5 Refrigerate the dough on the board for 15 minutes, or until it is firm enough to cut. Cut the dough into shapes using assorted gingerbread people cutters. Press any remaining dough together. Re-roll and cut out into shapes.

6 Bake for 10–12 minutes, or until lightly browned. Cool the biscuits on the trays, then decorate with the icing (frosting).

7 To make the icing, beat the egg white in a small bowl with electric beaters until soft peaks form. Gradually add the lemon juice and sifted icing sugar and beat until thick and creamy.

8 Divide the icing into several bowls and tint with food colourings. Spoon into small paper icing bags and use to decorate the biscuits.

These crunchy chocolate treats made with sultanas (golden raisins) and choc chips will be full of surprises for small partygoers.

Choc-chip crackles

90 g (3¼ oz/3 cups) puffed rice cereal

30 g (1 oz/¼ cup) unsweetened cocoa powder

150 g (5½ oz/1¼ cups) icing (confectioners') sugar

60 g (2¼ oz/½ cup) sultanas (golden raisins)

60 g (2¼ oz/⅔ cup) desiccated coconut

200 g (7 oz) Copha (white vegetable shortening), melted

60 g (2¼ oz/⅓ cup) dark choc chips

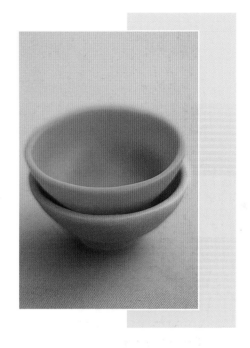

1 Line two 12-hole mini muffin tins with foil cases. Combine the puffed rice cereal, cocoa and sugar in a large bowl. Mix thoroughly, then stir in the sultanas and coconut. Stir in the melted shortening.

2 Spoon the mixture into the prepared muffin tins. Sprinkle with the choc chips. Refrigerate until set.

Prep time 20 minutes

Cooking time 5 minutes

Makes 24

Teddy birthday cake

445 g (15¾ oz) unsalted butter,
  softened

350 g (12 oz/1½ cups) caster
  (superfine) sugar

1 tablespoon natural vanilla extract

6 eggs, lightly beaten

550 g (1 lb 4 oz/4⅓ cups) self-raising
  flour

250 ml (9 fl oz/1 cup) milk

1½ quantities buttercream, from
  recipe on page 154

30 g (1 oz/¼ cup) unsweetened
  cocoa powder

Decoration

5 x 5 cm (2 inch) jam rollettes
  (mini jelly rolls)

2 round chocolate biscuits (cookies)

2 milk chocolate drops

1 white marshmallow, halved

liquorice pieces

1 red jellybean

Prep time 1 hour

Cooking time 35–40 minutes

Makes 1 cake

An old-fashioned butter cake makes good sense as a birthday cake for toddlers— particularly when it's made into a teddy bear!

1 Preheat the oven to 180°C (350°F/Gas 4). Grease and line the bases of two 18 cm (7 inch) round cake tins and a 1 litre (35 fl oz/4 cup) basin.

2 To make the cake, beat the butter and sugar until light and creamy. Add the vanilla extract and eggs one at a time, beating well after each addition. Fold in the sifted flour alternately with the milk until smooth.

3 Divide the cake mix evenly among the three tins and bake for 35–40 minutes, or until a skewer inserted into the centre comes out clean. Cool for 5 minutes, then turn out onto a wire rack to cool.

4 Spread the top of one round cake with some buttercream. Sandwich the round cakes together. Cut away the top and bottom edges of the cake sandwich to form a slight ball shape. This will be the fat body. Sit the pudding-shaped cake on top. Secure with skewers. Trim a diagonal slice around the bottom edge of the pudding for a neck.

5 Cut a diagonal slice off the end of four rollettes and attach them to the body with skewers to form the arms and legs. Cut a slice off the remaining rollette and attach it to the centre of the face with a skewer to form the snout. For ears, make two slits on the top of each side of the head, then push a round biscuit (cookie) into each.

6 Put 4 tablespoons of the buttercream in a bowl. Add the cocoa to the remainder and beat well. With a palette knife, spread the chocolate icing over the body, arms and legs (reserving a tablespoon for piping). Ice the tummy, snout and ears with the white buttercream.

7 For the eyes, stick a chocolate drop on each marshmallow half with icing. Use liquorice for the lips and nose and a jellybean for the mouth. Ice paw marks on the arms and legs with reserved chocolate icing.

Food allergy & intolerance

Contrary to its name, buckwheat is not related to wheat, so it is a gluten-free grain. Free of egg, dairy, gluten, nut and soy.

Buckwheat pancakes

130 g (4¾ oz/1 cup) buckwheat flour

1 egg, or equivalent egg replacer

185 ml (6 fl oz/¾ cup) water

canola oil, for greasing

125 ml (4 fl oz/½ cup) maple syrup

Prep time 10 minutes

Cooking time 20 minutes

Makes 16–20 pancakes

1 Sift the flour into a bowl and make a well in the centre. Add the combined egg or egg replacer and water. Beat with a wooden spoon until well combined and smooth. Pour the batter into a vessel with a pouring lip.

2 Brush a 20 cm (8 inch) frying pan with oil and heat over medium heat. Pour in just enough batter to thinly cover the bottom of the pan. When the top of the pancake starts to set, turn it over with a spatula and cook for a further 30 seconds. Transfer to a plate. Repeat with the remaining pancake batter, greasing the pan between batches. Serve with a drizzle of maple syrup.

Rice is an important source of energy-giving carbohydrates, ideal for small, food-sensitive tummies. Free of egg, dairy, gluten, nut and soy.

Rolled rice porridge

50 g (1¾ oz/½ cup) rolled rice or rice flakes
golden syrup, or maple syrup, to serve
peeled and chopped pear, to serve
pear juice (see page 183), to serve

1 Combine the rolled rice or rice flakes and 500 ml (17 fl oz/2 cups) boiling water in a saucepan. Cover with a lid and simmer over medium heat for 20 minutes, or until soft and creamy. Serve topped with golden or maple syrup, chopped pear and pear juice.

hint If you'd like a sweeter porridge, try adding a little pear juice in place of the water. You'll need to bring it to the boil before using it.

creamy rice porridge For a deliciously creamy taste, make the porridge with a non-dairy alternative, such as rice drink. Bring 500 ml (17 fl oz/2 cups) rice drink to the boil in a saucepan, then proceed with the recipe.

Prep time 5 minutes
Cooking time 20 minutes
Serves 4

If citrus fruits are off the menu, then potatoes become a good alternative source of vitamin C for your toddler. This recipe has more than their daily needs in one serve. Free of egg, dairy, gluten, nut and soy.

Potato & leek fritters

1.25 kg (2 lb 12 oz) white-skinned
   potatoes

1 leek, washed

2 eggs, lightly beaten, or equivalent
   egg replacer

1 tablespoon rice flour

2 tablespoons canola oil

Prep time 15 minutes

Cooking time 20 minutes

Serves 4–6

1 Peel and grate the potatoes. Pat the potato dry and put in a bowl. Finely chop the white part of the leek and add it to the bowl with the potato. Add the eggs or egg replacer and rice flour. Mix until combined.

2 Heat the oil in a large non-stick frying pan, Drop tablespoons of the mixture into the pan—you may need to cook the fritters in batches. Fry on each side for a few minutes or until golden brown. Serve hot or cold either on their own or with baked beans.

hints Use plain brushed potatoes. Red-skinned and new potatoes have moderate levels of natural flavour substances. Peeled potato will discolour if left to stand for too long.

Legumes such as chickpeas are a low-chemical source of vegetable protein as well as iron and the B vitamin folic acid. Free of egg, dairy, gluten, nut and soy.

Chickpea dip

125 g (4½ oz) tin chickpeas, rinsed and drained
¼ teaspoon citric acid (see hints)
60 ml (2 fl oz/¼ cup) pear juice (see page 183)
2 garlic cloves, crushed
2 tablespoons canola oil

1 Combine the chickpeas, citric acid, pear juice, garlic, oil and 2 tablespoons of water in a food processor. Process until smooth—the mixture should be the consistency of thick mayonnaise.

2 Scoop into a bowl and serve with crispy wafer biscuits (see the recipe opposite), chilled sticks of soft or blanched vegetables, such as celery or carrot, or fresh pieces of pide (Turkish/flat bread).

hints If tin chickpeas are unavailable, soak 50 g (1¾ oz/¼ cup) dried chickpeas in cold water overnight, then drain. Place in a saucepan with water and bring to the boil. Reduce the heat and simmer for about 2½ hours, or until tender. Drain well and proceed with the recipe. Citric acid is used as it is more likely to be tolerated than lemon juice or vinegar. It can be found at some supermarkets and health food stores.

chickpea & cashew dip To add a delicious nutty flavour to the above dip, process 115 g (4 oz/¾ cup) cashew nuts to a smooth paste in a small food processor and add it to the chickpea mixture.

Prep time 15 minutes
Cooking time Nil
Makes 250g (9 oz /1 cup)

These crisp wafers will put your mind at rest if you need to be certain about low-chemical snacks for your toddler. Free of egg, dairy, gluten, nut and soy.

Crispy wafer biscuits

175 g (6 oz/1 cup) rice flour

125 g (4½ oz/1 cup) cornflour (cornstarch)

40g (1½ oz/½ cup) rice bran

2 tablespoons canola oil, plus extra for greasing

Prep time 10 minutes
Cooking time 25 minutes
Makes 40

1 To make the biscuits (crackers), preheat the oven to 200°C (400°F/Gas 6). Lightly oil two 30 x 25 cm (12 x 10 inch) Swiss roll tins (jelly roll tins).

2 Combine the dry ingredients in a bowl, make a well in the centre and add 185 ml (6 fl oz/¾ cup) water combined with the oil. Mix until well combined.

3 Divide the mixture into two portions. Press each portion of dough into a prepared tin and bake for 20–25 minutes. Allow to cool in the tin. Turn out, break into pieces and store in an airtight container for up to 2 days.

hint If you'd like more evenly-shaped biscuits, score the dough in the tins with a knife before you bake them, then the biscuits will easily break along the score lines once they're cooked.

Small chicken pieces are easy-to-eat protein food for growing children. They are great served as a meal or a snack. Free of egg, dairy, gluten, nut and soy.

Glazed drumettes

16 chicken drumettes (see hint)

80 ml (2½ fl oz/⅓ cup) golden syrup (dark corn syrup)

60 ml (2 fl oz/¼ cup) pear juice (see page 183)

1 tablespoon canola oil

Prep time 20 minutes + overnight marinating

Cooking time 25 minutes

Serves 4

1 Put the drumettes in a shallow non-metallic dish. Combine the remaining ingredients and pour over the drumettes, making sure they are coated all over. Marinate overnight, turning occasionally.

2 Preheat the oven to 180°C (350°F/Gas 4). Transfer the drumettes and marinade to a baking tin. Bake for 20–25 minutes, turning frequently during cooking and brushing with the pan juices. If the pan juices start to overbrown, add a small amount of water or stock until syrupy. Serve hot or cold.

hint Chicken drumettes are available from most supermarkets and chicken shops. They are simply the wing with the tip removed and the flesh scraped back away from the bone and turned inside out.

glazed chicken with garlic & poppy seeds For added flavour, add 2 finely chopped spring onions (scallions), 2 crushed garlic cloves and 1 tablespoon poppy seeds to the golden syrup marinade. Follow the method as above.

Fish is good source of protein for growing toddlers. Its omega-3 fats are also great brain food. Free of egg, dairy, gluten, nut and soy.

Fish patties

700 g (1 lb 9 oz) white-skinned potatoes, quartered

2 tablespoons canola oil

500 g (1 lb 2 oz) boneless white fish fillets

1 leek, halved lengthways, chopped (white part only)

2 garlic cloves, crushed

30 g (1 oz/¼ cup) chopped spring onions (scallions)

iceberg lettuce leaves, to serve

pear chutney (see page 177), to serve

Prep time 20 minutes + 1 hour chilling

Cooking time 25 minutes

Serves 4

1 Put the potato into a large saucepan. Cover with cold water and bring to the boil. Boil for 15 minutes, or until the potato is tender. Drain well. Mash with a potato masher or fork.

2 Meanwhile, heat 2 teaspoons of the oil in a large non-stick frying pan over medium heat. Add the fish fillets and cook for 3–4 minutes on each side, or until cooked. Set side to cool.

3 Flake the fish with a fork. Heat another 2 teaspoons of the oil in the same frying pan over medium heat. Cook the leek and garlic, stirring often, for 5–6 minutes, or until the leek softens. Set aside on a plate. Wipe the pan clean with paper towels.

4 Combine the mashed potato, flaked fish, leek mixture and spring onion in a large bowl and mix thoroughly. Shape into eight patties and put on a plate. Cover and refrigerate for 1 hour.

5 Heat the remaining oil in the frying pan over medium heat. Cook the patties for 3–4 minutes on each side, or until lightly golden and heated through. Serve with lettuce leaves and pear chutney.

Not only are these sausages low-chemical, they are also lower in fat and salt than most commercially-made sausages. Free of egg, dairy, gluten, nut and soy.

Continental chicken sausages

750 g (1 lb 10 oz) minced (ground) chicken

2 eggs, lightly beaten, or equivalent egg replacer

20 g (¾ oz/1 cup) puffed rice cereal, finely crushed

1 tablespoon finely snipped chives

1 garlic clove, crushed

2 spring onions (scallions), finely chopped

1–1.25 litres (35–44 fl oz/4–5 cups) chicken stock (see low-chemical recipe on page 187)

1 tablespoon canola oil

Prep time 20 minutes + 1 hour chilling

Cooking time 20 minutes

Serves 4

1 Combine the chicken, eggs or egg replacer, puffed rice, chives, garlic and spring onions in a large bowl. Using your hands, mix and knead the mixture until completely combined.

2 Divide the mixture into eight even portions. Using wet hands, shape each portion into a sausage shape. Put on a large plate, cover with plastic wrap and refrigerate for 1 hour.

3 Put the chicken stock into a large saucepan and bring to the boil. Reduce the heat and bring to a simmer. Add the sausages to the simmering stock. Cover and cook for 10–15 minutes, or until the sausages are cooked through. Remove the sausages from the stock with a slotted spoon and pat dry on paper towels.

4 Heat the oil in a large frying pan over medium heat and add the sausages. Cook, turning often, until browned all over.

hint Minced (ground) chicken is available from chicken speciality shops and some supermarkets. It can be made at home by processing boneless, skinless chicken breasts or thighs.

chicken & carrot sausages Add 1 small finely grated carrot to the chicken mixture before dividing into portions, then proceed with the recipe above.

Rich in energy-giving carbohydrates from the pasta, this recipe also provides the minerals iron, zinc and potassium, as well as vitamin C and beta-carotene. Free of egg, dairy, gluten, nut and soy.

Vegetable & veal pasta

1½ tablespoons canola oil

1 leek, halved, washed and thinly sliced (white part only)

100 g (3½ oz) swede (rutabaga), chopped

100 g (3½ oz) white-skinned potatoes, chopped

2 garlic cloves, crushed

400 g (14 oz) cabbage, core removed and shredded

500 g (1 lb 2 oz) minced (ground) lean veal

2 teaspoons cornflour (cornstarch)

375 ml (13 fl oz/1½ cups) veal stock (see low-chemical recipe on page 187)

375 g (13 oz) rice pasta

Prep time 20 mins

Cooking time 25 mins

Serves 4

1 Heat 1 tablespoon of the oil in a large non-stick frying pan over medium heat. Add the leek, swede and potato. Cook, stirring often, for 5–6 minutes, or until the vegetables are almost tender. Add the garlic, cabbage and 2 tablespoons water. Cover and cook for a further 7–8 minutes, or until the cabbage is tender. Remove the vegetables from the pan.

2 Heat the remaining oil in the pan over high heat. Add the veal and cook, stirring for 3–4 minutes or until well browned. Combine the cornflour with a little of the stock in a bowl then add the remaining stock and a little salt. Add the stock mixture to the veal with the vegetables and stir until boiling. Reduce the heat and simmer for 2–3 minutes or until the sauce thickens.

3 Meanwhile, cook the pasta following the packet instructions until *al dente*. Drain and return to the pan.

4 Divide the pasta among four serving plates. Top with the meat and vegetable mixture and serve immediately.

hint If your child can tolerate gluten, pasta sauce can also be served with wheat spaghetti or other wheat pasta.

This recipe provides vitamin C and beta-carotene from the peas, and calcium and phosphorus from the yoghurt. Contains dairy. Free of egg, gluten, nut and soy.

Pea purée with yoghurt

310 g (11 oz/2 cups) frozen peas

1 large handful flat-leaf (Italian) parsley, chopped

6 spring onions (scallions), chopped

125 ml (4 fl oz/½ cup) pear juice (see page 183)

½ teaspoon citric acid

250 g (9 oz/1 cup) plain yoghurt

1 Bring a saucepan of water to the boil, then add the peas, parsley and spring onions. Cook for 2–3 minutes, or until the peas are green and tender.

2 Strain and reserve 80 ml (2½ fl oz/⅓ cup) of the cooking liquid. Purée the pea mixture, reserved cooking liquid, pear juice and citric acid in a food processor or blender. Return to the saucepan and cook over low heat until the sauce is warmed through. Remove the pan from the heat and stir in the yoghurt. Do not reheat once you have added the yoghurt or the purée will curdle.

3 Serve with lamb cutlets or over baked or boiled potatoes.

Prep time 10 minutes

Cooking time 5 minutes

Serves 4

Rich in protein and healthy fats, this is perfect growing food for kids. Free of egg, dairy, gluten, nut and soy.

Rice-crumbed fish with wedges

2 eggs, or equivalent egg replacer

2 tablespoons rice drink

60 g (2¼ oz/½ cup) soy-free, gluten-free (all-purpose) flour

70 g (2½ oz/1 cup) rice crumbs

four 125 g (4½ oz) boneless white fish fillets

canola oil spray

iceberg lettuce leaves, to serve

pear-chutney (see page 177), to serve

Wedges

1 kg (2 lb 4 oz) white-skinned potatoes, cut into wedges

canola oil spray

Prep time 20 minutes

Cooking time 50 minutes

Serves 4

1 Preheat the oven to 220°C (425°F/ Gas 7). Line two large baking trays with baking paper.

2 Combine the egg or egg replacer and rice drink in a shallow dish. Put the flour and rice crumbs in two separate shallow dishes. Dip the fish in the flour, then the egg mixture and lastly in the rice crumbs to coat well. Lay the crumbed fish in a single layer on one of the lined trays. Refrigerate until required.

3 Put the potato wedges in a large bowl. Spray the wedges with oil. Toss to coat. Spread over the other lined tray.

4 Bake the potato wedges for 30 minute, turning once. Put the wedges on the lower shelf of the oven. Remove the fish from the refrigerator, then spray both sides of the fish lightly with oil. Add the fish to the top shelf and cook for 20 minutes, turning halfway though, or until the fish is cooked and the wedges are crispy.

breadcrumb-coated fish Commercial breadcrumbs always contain preservatives. You can make your own by putting preservative-free bread slices on baking trays and slowly baking until crisp. Process in a food processor and store in an airtight jar. To make breadcrumb-coated fish, combine 1 egg and 1 tablespoon milk in a bowl, put 60 g (2¼ oz/½ cup) plain (all-purpose) flour in a separate bowl and 165 g (5 ¾ oz/2 cups) home-made breadcrumbs in a third bowl. Dip the fish first in the flour, then the egg wash and lastly in the breadcrumbs. Follow the cooking method in the recipe above.

These fritters are an excellent source of fibre and provide good amounts of protein and iron. Free of egg, dairy, gluten, nut and soy.

Chickpea fritters

2 tablespoons canola oil

4 spring onions (scallions), sliced

2 garlic cloves, chopped

600 g (1 lb 5 oz) tin chickpeas, rinsed and drained

1 egg, or egg equivalent replacer

pear chutney (see page 177), to serve

small cos (romaine) lettuce leaves, to serve

crusty gluten-free bread, to serve

Prep time 20 minutes

Cooking time 10 minutes

Makes 6

1 Heat 2 teaspoons of the oil in a large non-stick frying pan over medium heat. Add the spring onions and garlic and cook, stirring, for 1–2 minutes, or until the spring onion softens.

2 Put the chickpeas and spring onion mixture in a food processor. Process until the mixture starts to hold together. Transfer to a bowl and mix in the egg or egg replacer. Using your hands, shape the mixture into six even fritters.

3 Heat the remaining oil in a large non-stick frying pan over medium heat. Add the chickpea fritters (cook in two batches if necessary) and cook for 2 minutes on each side, or until golden. Serve with chutney, lettuce crusty gluten-free bread.

Foods with lots of flavour are often the ones food-sensitive kids can't have. This recipe is an exception. Free of egg, dairy, gluten, nut and soy.

Pear chutney

820 g (1 lb 13 oz) tin pear halves in syrup

125 g (4½ oz/⅔ cup) soft brown sugar

1½ teaspoons citric acid

1 teaspoon ground sea salt

Prep time 10 minutes
Cooking time 25 minutes
Makes 375 g (13 oz/1½ cups)

1 Drain and chop the pears, reserving the syrup.

2 Pour the syrup into a saucepan. Bring to the boil and boil until the mixture is reduced by half.

3 Add the pears, sugar, citric acid and salt. Reduce the heat. Allow to simmer for about 10–15 minutes, or until the mixture is thick.

4 Spoon into hot, sterilised jars. Seal, label and date. Once opened, store in the refrigerator and use within 3 weeks.

Using healthy fats and natural ingredients, these sausage rolls make a nutritious snack for any time of the day. Free of egg, dairy, gluten, nut and soy.

Gluten-free sausage rolls

canola oil, for greasing

400 g (14 oz) white-skinned potatoes, roughly chopped

1 tablespoon canola oil

125 g (4½ oz/1 cup) soy-free, gluten-free self-raising flour

½ teaspoon gluten-free baking powder

½ teaspoon ground sea salt

1 egg, or equivalent egg replacer

Filling

300 g (10½ oz) minced (ground) chicken or veal

1 egg, or equivalent egg replacer

40 g (1½ oz/½ cup) gluten-free fresh breadcrumbs

1 spring onion (scallion), finely chopped

½ teaspoon ground sea salt

1 egg, or equivalent egg replacer, for brushing

Prep time 45 minutes

Cooking time 25 minutes

Makes 18

1 Preheat the oven to 200°C (400°F/Gas 6). Lightly grease two baking trays. Boil or steam the potato for 15 minutes, or until tender. Drain and return to the pan and mash until smooth. You will need about 235 g (8 ½ oz/1 cup) mashed potato for this recipe.

2 Combine the mashed potato and oil in a large bowl. Add the sifted dry ingredients and egg and mix to a smooth dough. Knead on a lightly floured surface until smooth. Roll the dough into a 35 cm (14 inch) square, trimming the edges. Cut the dough evenly into three strips.

3 To make the filling, combine the meat, egg or egg replacer, breadcrumbs, spring onion and salt in a bowl. Add 1 tablespoon water and mix well to combine. Divide the filling into three portions and, using wet hands, form each portion into thin rolls. Lay the filling along the centre of the pastry strips and brush the extra egg along the edges. Wrap the pastry around the filling, placing them seam side down. Repeat with the remaining filling and pastry.

4 Brush the rolls with the remaing egg, then cut each roll into six pieces. Place the sausage rolls on the prepared trays, prick the tops with a fork and bake for 20–25 minutes, or until cooked through and golden.

hints Sausage rolls can be made a day in advance and kept in the refrigerator. When required, wrap the cooked sausage rolls in foil and reheat at 180°C (350°F/Gas 4) for 5–8 minutes. If your child can tolerate gluten, you can use commercial puff pastry with no added preservatives or antioxidants.

If dairy is allowed, serve these pikelets with pear yoghurt to make a calcium- and carbohydrate-rich snack. Contains egg. Free of dairy, gluten, nut and soy.

Gluten-free pikelets

85 g (3 oz/⅔ cup) soy-free, gluten-free (all-purpose) flour

½ teaspoon bicarbonate of soda (baking soda)

1 teaspoon cream of tartar

30 g (1 oz/⅓ cup) rice barn

2 eggs separated

1 tablespoon canola oil

canola oil spray, for greasing

Prep time 15 minutes

Cooking time 15 minutes

Makes about 24

1 To make the pikelets (griddle cakes), sift the flour, bicarbonate of soda and cream of tartar into a bowl. Mix in the rice bran. Make a well in the centre and stir in the combined egg yolks, oil and 25 0ml (9 fl oz/1 cup) water. Beat well until smooth.

2 Beat the egg whites until stuff peaks form, then fold into the batter using a large metal spoon.

3 Spray a non-stick frying pan lightly with oil and place over medium heat. Place 2 tablespoons of the mixture for each pikelet in the pan, allowing room for spreading. When the mixture starts to set and the bubbles burst, turn over and brown the other side. Repeat the process with the remaining mixture. Place the pikelets on a wire cake rack to cool. Serve with pear yoghurt, if desired (see recipe below).

hint Pikelets can be frozen and reheated briefly in a warm oven.

pear yoghurt To make pear yoghurt, combine 250 g (9 oz/1 cup) plain yogurt, ½ peeled and chopped pear and 2 teaspoons soft brown sugar.

With gluten-free flours available in most supermarkets, home-made muffins like these are easy to make. Free of egg, dairy, gluten, nut and soy.

Gluten-free pear muffins

canola oil, for greasing

250 g (9 oz/2 cups) soy-free, gluten-free self-rasing flour

2 teaspoons gluten-free baking powder

140 g (5 oz/¾ cup) soft brown sugar

170 ml (5½ fl oz/⅔ cup) rice drink

80 ml (2½ fl oz/⅓ cup) canola oil

2 eggs, or equivalent egg replacer

2 ripe pears (about 450 g /1 lb) peeled, cored and mashed

Prep time 15 minutes

Cooking time 20 minutes

Makes 12

1 Preheat the oven to 180°C (350°F/Gas 4). Lightly grease a 12-hole muffin tin with canola oil.

2 Sift the flour and baking powder into a large bowl and add the sugar. In a separate bowl, combine the rice drink, oil and eggs or egg replacer. Add the rice drink mixture and pears to the flour mixture. Use a large metal spoon to mix until just combined. Spoon the mixture into the muffin tin.

3 Bake for 18–20 minutes, or until a skewer inserted in the centre comes out clean. Leave for 5 minutes before turning onto a wire rack.

hint These muffins need to be eaten on the day they are made.

gluten-free banana muffins Replace pears with 2 large, ripe bananas, mashed.

gluten-free rhubarb muffins Replace the pears with ½ bunch rhubarb, washed and cut into 2 cm (¾ inch) long pieces. Increase the rice drink to 185 ml (6 fl oz/¾ cup).

This milkshake is rich in calcium and phosphorus, making it excellent for strong bones and teeth. Contains dairy. Free of egg, gluten, nut and soy.

Carob milkshake

1 tablespoon carob powder

1 tablespoon sugar

500 ml (17 fl oz/2 cups) milk, well chilled

40 g (1½ oz/¼ cup) finely chopped carob buttons

Prep time 5 minutes

Cooking time Nil

Serves 2

1 Dissolve the carob powder and sugar in 1 tablespoon hot water. Allow to cool.

2 Combine the milk and carob mixture by whisking and beating together. Pour into long glasses. Top with finely chopped carob buttons.

hint Ask your health food story whether their carob buttons contain dairy and/or soy.

This juice is easy to digest and a great source of fibre. It is best if diluted with equal parts of water for toddlers. Free of egg, dairy, gluten, nut and soy.

Pear juice

825 g (1 lb 13 oz) tin pear halves in syrup

1 Put the pears and syrup into a blender. Blend on high speed for 2–3 minutes, or until puréed.

2 Scoop the pear juice into a covered container and store in the refrigerator for up to 4 days.

hint Pear juice may be diluted with unflavoured mineral water or cooled, boiled tap water. Pear juice can also be used to naturally sweeten breakfast cereals such as porridge or muesli (granola).

Prep time 5 minutes
Cooking time Nil
Serves 4-6

Basics

Vegetable stock

1 tablespoon oil

1 brown onion, chopped

2 leeks, thickly sliced (white part only)

4 carrots, chopped

2 parsnips, chopped

4 celery stalks, leaves included, chopped

2 bay leaves

1 bouquet garni (see hint)

4 unpeeled garlic cloves

8 black peppercorns

1 Heat the oil in a large, heavy-based saucepan and add the onion, leek, carrot, parsnip and celery. Cover and cook for 5 minutes without colouring. Add 3 litres (105 fl oz/12 cups) water. Bring to the boil. Add the bay leaves, bouquet garni, garlic and peppercorns. Reduce the heat to low and simmer for 1 hour. Skim the froth from the surface of the stock regularly.

2 Strain the stock. Set aside to cool, then transfer to an airtight container. Store in the refrigerator for up to 2 days or in the freezer for up to 6 months.

hint To make your own bouquet garni, tie together with a string or wrap in a piece of cheesecloth (muslin) 4 sprigs parsley or chervil, 1 sprig fresh thyme and 1 bay leaf.

Makes 2.5 litres (87 fl oz/10 cups)

Low-chemical vegetable stock*

1 tablespoon canola oil

3 celery stalks, sliced

350 g (12 oz) chopped swede (rutabaga)

1 large leek, halved lengthways, chopped

3 garlic cloves, crushed

1 Heat canola oil in a large saucepan over medium heat. Add celery, swede (rutabaga), leek and garlic. Cook, stirring often, for 5–8 minutes, or until the vegetables turn golden in colour. Pour in 4.5 litres (157 fl oz/18 cups) water. Cover with a lid and bring to the boil. Simmer, partially covered, for 1½ hours, skimming the froth from the surface of the stock regularly.

2 Strain the stock. Set aside to cool, then transfer to an airtight container. Store in the refrigerator for up to 2 days or in the freezer for up to 6 months.

Makes 2.5 litres (87 fl oz/10 cups).

* Suitable for children with food intolerances requiring an elimination or low chemical diet

Chicken stock

2 kg (4 lb 8 oz) chicken bones

2 unpeeled brown onions, quartered

2 unpeeled carrots, chopped

2 celery stalks, leaves included, chopped

1 bouquet garni

12 black peppercorns

1 Put the chicken bones, onion, carrot, celery and 3.5 litres (122 fl oz/14 cups) water in a large, heavy-based saucepan. Bring slowly to the boil. Skim the surface as required and add the bouquet garni and peppercorns. Reduce the heat to low and simmer gently for 3 hours. Skim the froth from the surface regularly.

2 Strain the stock. Set aside to cool, then refrigerate until cold. Spoon off any fat that has set on the surface. Transfer to an airtight container. Store in the refrigerator for up to 2 days or in the freezer for up to 6 months.

Makes 2.5 litres (87 fl oz/10 cups)

Low-chemical chicken or veal stock*

500 g (1 lb 2 oz) chicken or veal bones

1 leek, roughly chopped

1 celery stalk, roughly chopped

1 carrot, roughly chopped

4 parsley stalks (without foliage)

1 Put chicken or veal bones in a large heavy-based saucepan. Add leek, celery, carrot and parsley stalks. Cover with water and bring to the boil, skimming the surface. Reduce the heat and simmer for about 1–1½ hours, uncovered.

2 Strain through a colander, then through a fine sieve. Remove any fat from the surface. Store in the refrigerator for up to 2 days or in the freezer for up to 6 months.

Makes 2.5 litres (87 fl oz/10 cups)

* Suitable for children with food intolerances requiring an elimination or low chemical diet

Beef stock

2 kg (4 lb 8 oz) beef bones

2 unpeeled carrots, chopped

2 unpeeled brown onions, quartered

2 tablespoons tomato paste (conentrated purée)

2 celery stalks, leaves included, chopped

1 bouquet garni

12 black peppercorns

1 Preheat the oven to 210°C (415°F/Gas 6–7). Put the bones in a baking tin and bake for 30 minutes, turning occasionally. Add the carrot and onion and cook for a further 20 minutes. Allow to cool.

2 Put the bones, onion and carrot in a large, heavy-based saucepan. Drain the excess fat from the baking tin and pour 250 ml (9 fl oz/1 cup) water into the tin. Stir to dissolve any pan juices, then add the liquid to the pan.

3 Add the tomato paste, celery and 2.5 litres (87 fl oz/10 cups) water. Bring to the boil, skimming the surface as required, and then add the bouquet garni and peppercorns. Reduce the heat to low and simmer gently for 4 hours. Skim the froth from the surface regularly.

4 Strain through a colander, then through a fine sieve. Remove any fat from the surface. Store in the refrigerator for up to 2 days or in the freezer for up to 6 months.

Makes about 1.75 litres (61 fl oz/7 cups)

Basic tomato sauce

1.5 kg (3 lb 5 oz) tomatoes

1 tablespoon olive oil

1 brown onion, finely chopped

2 garlic cloves, crushed

2 tablespoons tomato paste (concentrated purée)

1 teaspoon dried oregano

1 teaspoon dried basil

1 teaspoon sugar

1 Score a cross on the base of each tomato, place in a bowl of boiling water for about 10 seconds, then plunge into cold water and peel away the skin from the cross. Finely chop the flesh.

2 Heat the margarine in pan. Add the onion and cook, stirring, over medium heat for 3 minutes, or until soft. Add the garlic and cook for 1 minute. Add the tomato, tomato paste, oregano, basil and sugar. Bring to the boil, then reduce the heat and simmer for 20 minutes, or until the sauce has thickened slightly.

3 Store in an airtight container in the refrigerator for up to 2 days or in the freezer for up to 6 months.

Serves 4

White sauce

250 ml (9 fl oz/1 cup) milk
1 brown onion slice
1 bay leaf
6 peppercorns
30 g (1 oz) margarine
1 tablespoon plain (all-purpose) flour

1 Put the milk, onion, bay leaf and
peppercorns in a small saucepan. Bring
to the boil, remove from the heat and leave
to infuse for 10 minutes. Strain the milk,
discarding the flavourings.

2 Melt the butter in a small pan and stir in
the flour. Cook, stirring, for 1 minute until
the mixture is golden and bubbling. Remove
from the heat and gradually add the milk,
stirring until completely smooth. Return
to the heat and stir until the mixture boils.
Continue cooking for 1 minute, or until
thick. Remove from the heat and serve.

Serves 2–4

Barbecue dipping sauce

2 teaspoons oil
1 small brown onion, finely chopped
1 tablespoon malt vinegar
1 tablespoon soft brown sugar
**80 ml (2½ fl oz/⅓ cup) salt-reduced
tomato sauce (ketchup)**
1 tablespoon worcestershire sauce

1 Heat the oil in a small saucepan and cook
the onion over low heat for 3 minutes,
or until soft, stirring occasionally.

2 Add the remaining ingredients and bring to
the boil. Reduce the heat and simmer for
3 minutes, stirring occasionally. Serve warm
or at room temperature. Can be kept covered
and refrigerated for up to 1 week.

Serves 2–4

Index